Set in 11.5 on 13.5 centaur for
FOUR COURTS PRESS LTD
7 Malpas Street, Dublin 8, Ireland
e-mail: info@four-courts-press.ie
http://www.four-courts-press.ie
and in North America
FOUR COURTS PRESS
c/o ISBS, 920 N.E. 58th Street, Suite 300, Portland, OR 97213.

© the various authors and Four Courts Press 2005

A catalogue record for this title
is available from the British Library.

ISBN 1–85182–846–x hbk
ISBN 1–85182–869–9 pbk

Printed in Great Britain
by MPG Books, Bodmin, Cornwall

POLITICAL CENSORSHIP
AND THE
DEMOCRATIC STATE

The Irish Broadcasting Ban

Mary P. Corcoran & Mark O'Brien

EDITORS

FOUR COURTS PRESS

Everyone is in favour of free speech. Hardly a day passes without its being extolled, but some people's idea of it is that they are free to say what they like, but if anyone else says anything back, that is an outrage.

Winston Churchill

Contents

PART III   MEDIA, CENSORSHIP AND THE PUBLIC SPHERE

Contributors

Farrel Corcoran is professor of Communication at Dublin City University, where he has also served as Head of the School of Communications and Dean of the Faculty of Humanities. He was Chairman of RTÉ for five years and recently, with the support of a Government of Ireland Senior Fellowship, completed a major study of broadcasting that has just been published: *RTÉ and the gobalisation of Irish television* (2004).

Mary P. Corcoran is a senior lecturer in the Department of Sociology, NUI Maynooth. A graduate of Trinity College Dublin and Columbia University, New York, her research and teaching interests include ethnicity and migration, urban social change and professional media cultures. She is co-editor (with Michel Peillon) of *Ireland unbound: a turn of the century chronicle* (2002) and *Place and non-Place* (2004). Mary Corcoran has published widely in the field of sociology and is also an occasional commentator on radio and television.

Desmond Fisher was successively Deputy Head of News, Head of the Current Affairs Grouping and Director of Broadcasting Development in RTÉ between 1968 and 1983. He is a former editor of the *Catholic Herald* (London), and author of *The Church in transition* and *Broadcasting in Ireland* (1978) and has written extensively on the concept of the right to communicate.

Roy Greenslade, professor of Journalism, City University, London, is a former editor of the *Daily Mirror* and is a media commentator with the *Guardian* newspaper.

Michael D. Higgins is a Dáil Deputy for Galway West, a former Chairman of the Labour Party and a lecturer in Political Science and Sociology at NUI Galway. In 1992 he was the first recipient of the Sean McBride International Peace Medal of the International Peace Bureau for his work for human rights. In 1993 he was appointed Minister for the Arts, Culture and the Gaeltacht. His first collection of poetry *The Betrayal* was published in 1990 and was followed in 1993 by *The Season of Fire*.

Colum Kenny is a barrister and journalist. A former employee of RTÉ and member of the IRTC and Broadcasting Commission of Ireland between 1988 and 1993, Dr Kenny is today chairperson of the Masters in Journalism course at

Dublin City University. His books include a pioneering study of professionalization, *Tristram Kennedy and the revival of Irish legal training, 1835-1885* (1996) and an overview of Britain's nuclear reprocessing plant, *Fearing Sellafield* (2003).

Ed Moloney is a journalist and author who has written for the *Washington Post*, *The Economist* and *The Guardian*. He was elected Irish Journalist of the Year in 1999 and has spent two decades writing about the IRA, first as Northern Ireland Editor of the *Irish Times* and then as Northern Editor of the *Sunday Tribune*. He gained unprecedented access to the IRA while researching his recent book *A secret history of the IRA* (2002).

Conor Cruise O'Brien served as a diplomat at the United Nations between 1955 and 1960 and as UN representative to Katanga in 1961. He was Vice-Chancellor of Ghana University between 1962 and 1965 and was also Albert Schweitzer professor of Humanities at New York University. He served as Minister for Posts and Telegraphs between 1973 and 1977 and as editor-in-chief of *The Observer* between 1977 and 1980. He is the author of *States of Ireland* (1972) and *Herod: reflections on political violence* (1978).

Mark O'Brien is a lecturer in sociology and media studies in the School of Communications, Dublin City University. A former chairperson of the MA in Political Communications, he is the author of *De Valera, Fianna Fáil and the* Irish Press: *the truth in the news?* (2001).

Helen Shaw is managing director of Athena Media Ltd, a multi-media production and consultancy company. She reported from Northern Ireland for the *Irish Times* in the mid 1980s and returned to Belfast ten years later as a news editor for BBC Northern Ireland. She won a Gold Sony award for her work there. She was Director of Radio, RTÉ and a member of the RTÉ Board until September 2002, when she was awarded a one-year fellowship at Harvard University researching media globalization.

Alex White is a barrister and former RTÉ producer. He is a graduate of Trinity College Dublin and the King's Inns, and was called to the Bar in 1987. He joined RTÉ in 1984 as a current affairs producer and was editor of *The Gay Byrne Show* between 1990 and 1994. During his time in RTÉ he was an active trade unionist and a leading opponent of Section 31. One of the applicants to the European Commission on Human Rights in the case of *Purcell v. Ireland*, he was also a founding member of the 'Let in the Light' campaign.

Foreword

ROY GREENSLADE

Some time in the mid-1970s I attended a National Union of Journalists annual delegate meeting and spoke in favour of a motion that called on the Irish government to repeal Section 31. Later, at lunch, a white-faced man appeared at my table and, after rapidly explaining that he was a journalist on a local newspaper in a Surrey town with a huge British army barracks, he spread out a selection of photographs showing the bloody scenes following a Belfast bombing. He was obviously in a highly emotional state. 'That's what you want, is it?' he said, his voice rising with each sentence. 'That's what you're supporting, is it? You go on about free speech but the people in these pictures don't have free speech. They don't have free anything. You're so naive. You don't know what you're talking about. You're doing the bombers' work for them'.

There was much more in similar vein as I sought to argue my case. I tried to point out that it was perfectly logical to oppose Section 31's denial of free speech and, at the same time, oppose the violence of the Provisional IRA. Indeed, it was plausible to contend that violence was a more likely consequence of banning IRA supporters from the airwaves than if they were allowed to broadcast. In the heat of the moment, I called the pictures 'irrelevant' (a word I've always wished I could retract), prompting him to lose his temper as he thrust one of the photos – showing a mangled body – inches from my face. I changed tack. Since it was generally acknowledged that one of terrorism's main aims was to engender a disproportionate response from the authorities, I suggested that the imposition of censorship was the desired result of the terrorists.[1] To ban them would prove counter-productive. By now, a crowd had gathered and, unsurprisingly since they were all union activists, most of them joined in. The resulting hubbub effectively ended any (already frail) possibility of conducting a rational dialogue in which, doubtless, many other points would have been raised. So my critic, as upset as I was by the intervention, gathered up his pictures and left.

Though that confrontation probably lasted no more than ten minutes, I dwelt on it often in the years afterwards. The man, whose name I didn't catch and who never contacted me again, was clearly sincere. His argument was, in essence, similar to that of Conor Cruise O'Brien and, some time later, Margaret Thatcher: by

---

1 For the purposes of this discussion, I am accepting that the IRA's actions amounted to terrorism. The 'one man's terrorist is another man's freedom fighter' debate is a separate matter.

flouting the rule of law and declaring war on a democratic society terrorists for-
feit the rights enjoyed by that society. Not only did the terrorists and their political supporters have no right to the 'oxygen of publicity', the public should be
protected from such views: people had a 'right' not to hear them. Seen from the
perspective of 2004 the imposition of Section 31 seems like a bad dream. Did a
democratic state really censor its public service broadcaster for over twenty years?
Did that state's political leaders genuinely believe that their draconian legislation
would succeed in eradicating the viewpoint of a group that was, regardless of the
low level of support for violence, espousing the deeply-held political ambitions
of a majority of the population? Did the broadcaster's senior journalistic staff,
whose primary function should have been the promotion of freedom of speech
and freedom of information, believe they were acting for the public benefit when
complying so rigorously with Section 31? Do any of those people responsible for
implementing and/or condoning censorship – be they journalist, politician,
judge or broadcasting executive – now believe they were correct?

These questions have assumed a new relevance in the light of the so-called
'war on terror' instituted by the United States, a war that has been backed so
enthusiastically by Britain and, tacitly, by the Irish government. Having assumed
the mantle of patriotism, a largely compliant U.S. media has engaged in the kind
of self-censorship that has obviated the need for a Section 31. But the issues in
both cases are similar, and they touch on the often-fraught relationship between
the state and the media in hundreds of countries across the globe. Can censorship of any kind ever be justified?

What is so important about this book is the way in which its detailed analysis of a single instance raises universal concerns. One of its main values is that it
considers broadcast censorship from a variety of perspectives, thus offering a
coherent and comprehensive account. Better still, some of the writers played key
roles in the implementation of Section 31, either as policy-makers or bureaucrat-
ic policemen, while others struggled to circumvent its stifling and often absurd
demands. Whether one agrees or not with Conor Cruise O'Brien's defence of
Section 31 (and I certainly do not), his justification for its imposition could hardly be better argued. Clearly, he believed that broadcasting, as distinct from the
press, had a special effect on its audience and that this effect was compounded
by RTÉ's position as the nation's public service broadcaster. Broadcasting, he contended, 'has by far the most immediate impact on people and situations' and 'by
far the greatest capacity to generate emotion'. Therefore, despite the low level of
public support for the IRA, viewers might be influenced by 'a certain miasma of
glamour'. There are remarkable parallels between O'Brien's viewpoint and that of
Alastair Campbell, former director of communications for Britain's prime minister, Tony Blair, who concentrated most of his energies while in office on trying

to control the BBC's output. For both men, and their hosts of political supporters, a public service broadcaster is considered to be the most influential media
organization.

They view it as having a special relationship with the public that derives, in
part, from the fact that viewers and listeners fund it through a mandatory licence
fee. They also believe, despite their protestations to the contrary (itself an artful
deception), that the public inevitably perceive a public service broadcaster as an
organ of the state and therefore endowed with a quasi-official status, lending it
an authority and credibility that is not replicated by commercial broadcasters and
partisan, privately-owned newspapers. In other words, according to the O'Brien-
Campbell thesis, people are more likely to believe what they see and hear on RTÉ
or the BBC. O'Brien argued that Sinn Féin spokespersons, simply by appearing
on news bulletins and current affairs programmes, were given a spurious legitimacy. Campbell's concern was slightly different: his constant complaint was that
critical, interpretative reports broadcast by supposedly neutral BBC journalists
legitimised anti-government 'propaganda'. This culminated, of course, in the
Gilligan-Kelly affair that led to the Hutton Inquiry.

In both instances – the imposition of Section 31 in Ireland and the Hutton
debacle in Britain – the underlying message from the censors (or would-be censors) was the same: broadcasting is the most powerful and influential medium
and must, therefore, be controlled. But the censors were, and are, wrong. In a
multi-media world, people consume the totality of the media. Indeed, they hardly need to consume it actively. News is ambient and they receive it as if by osmo-
sis. In spite of Section 31, the Irish people knew not only the activities of the IRA
but the reasons for those activities. With the admitted advantage of hindsight, it
is perfectly plausible to argue that the only thing the broadcasting ban achieved
was to delay the move away from militarism by republicans towards politics. The
censorship made it more difficult for Sinn Féin to convince the IRA, which was
conscious of being officially marginalised (and which, quite possibly, it relished),
to curb its violent campaign. One of saddest features of Section 31 was the failure of the majority of journalists to make a principled stand against it, probably
because they tacitly agreed with its aims and were happy to comply.

That's another reason why this book, and the concerns it raises, could not be
more timely when the so-called 'war on terror' threatens all our freedoms. Terrorism may be a threat to democracy, but it is a greater threat when democracy
bends its knee to the terrorist. It may appear unduly liberal to those who revert
so willingly to autocracy in the face of violence, but there is, in the end, no substitute for understanding. Reactionaries threaten democracy by shooting first and
asking questions later. It is incumbent on democrats to do the opposite: to ask
'why' and to go on asking 'why'. Of course, to do that, they require information

and if free speech is suppressed they cannot hope to make informed decisions. That is why censorship imposed in the name of democracy can never be justified.

Introduction

MARY P. CORCORAN AND MARK O'BRIEN

We hear a lot today about the problem of information overload. There are so many media platforms, carrying a multiplicity of messages, representing a multiplicity of viewpoints and so little time to absorb and make sense of them all. If you live anywhere in the 'wired' world, the flow of signs and messages is continuous and ubiquitous. As such, it is becoming less and less possible to imagine a world wherein information is successfully restricted or suppressed. And yet the urge to censor, to control the flow of information, remains a perennial objective even within the most liberal of liberal democracies. The urge to censor today centres very much on the flow of information and images on the internet. But, in many countries around the globe, governments seek to censor all channels of political communication.

Not so long ago, political censorship as a mechanism for effecting a particular political objective was embedded in the policy frameworks of the Republic of Ireland, Northern Ireland and Great Britain. The aim of this book is to present a case study of the genesis, implementation and effects of political censorship in a modern democratic state. Taking the case study of the broadcasting ban on interviews with members of proscribed organisations in force in Ireland from 1971 to 1994, we present a critical study of journalistic practice in 'crisis' or conflict situations. Journalistic, sociological, legal and political perspectives on the broadcasting ban have been assembled here to provide a fresh and timely insight into the wider issue of the subordination of the media within the structures of state power.

In the post-September 11th world, and in the shadow of war and ongoing hostilities in various corners of the globe, western states have become increasingly preoccupied with national security. In the United States we have seen the unprecedented introduction of legislation that limits civil liberties, and in the United Kingdom we have witnessed renewed attempts by government to shape the news agenda. Who could have imagined that in the twenty-first century armed air marshals would be drafted in to secure civilian flights? Or that federal agents no longer need to demonstrate probable cause in order to look into the business records of, among other places, libraries and bookstores?[1] Or that the BBC would find itself shaken to its foundations in the wake of its fractious encounters with Downing Street over coverage of the war in Iraq?

1 USA Patriot Act 2001, Section 215.

In such a climate, the relative openness or closure of a given national media system clearly has consequences for the operation of the public sphere: that space wherein citizens gain access to information and are empowered to form opinions. However, the operation of a range of subtle and not so subtle constraints in the sphere of political communication means that in the contemporary era 'the range of effective voices in the public sphere is an outcome of battles over information management in society'.[2] If we are to contain the erosion of voices in the public sphere, we need to analyze and reflect upon the conditions under which such erosion is instigated by the state, becomes widely legitimated, and produces a chilling effect. We need to develop a critical understanding of the information management strategies being developed in the modern democratic state. The contributions in this book focus on the implementation, subsequent repeal and effects of political censorship in the Irish state from 1971 to 2004, the tenth anniversary of the lifting of the broadcasting ban. Taken together, the various perspectives advanced offer a valuable case study of the workings of political and ideological constraints and their constitutive role in both the broadcast journalist's self-understanding, and the perceptions and opinions of the media audience.

For over two decades Irish broadcast journalists were required to refrain from broadcasting any interview or report of an interview with spokespersons for the IRA, Sinn Féin, Republican Sinn Féin, the Ulster Defence Association, the INLA and any organisation that was a proscribed grouping in Northern Ireland under the terms of the Northern Ireland (Emergency Provisions) Act of 1978. This constraint affected the national broadcaster's coverage of Northern Ireland, and resulted in numerous court cases, the imprisonment of one journalist and the sacking of another, accusations of bias and self-censorship among broadcast journalists, and allegations of excessive political interference in the working of the broadcast media. It is timely, ten years after the repeal of the censorship provision, and in light of the peace process in Northern Ireland, to revisit the contentious issue of political censorship and the modern state. This collection of essays presents a unique opportunity to reflect on political censorship, how it is conceived, implemented, legitimated and at times, resisted. Furthermore, it provides insights into the longer-term effects of political censorship – even when the constraints themselves have been removed. For this reason, this case study tells a story that is pertinent for any citizen living in any state, democratic or otherwise, in the present day.

The book is divided into three parts. In the first part, 'Censorship and the State', we present an edited version of Conor Cruise O'Brien's Seanad address in March 1975 in which he set out the rationale for Section 31 of the Broadcasting Authority (Amendment) Act 1976. He argues that the democratic state has the

2 Scheslinger, P., 'From production to propaganda?' *Media, Culture and Society* 11 (3) 1989, 283–306.

right, in certain circumstances, to introduce repressive legislation in order to protect the public good. The speech is very much a product of its time, and reflects the widespread fear that the institutions of the state in the Republic were fragile and could be undermined either by armed conspiracies, or by the legitimation of the aims and objectives of armed groups in Irish society. To safeguard the country against these threats, the terms under which the national broadcaster covered Northern Ireland needed to be tightened.

Alex White sets out the legal background to the introduction of the 1976 legislation, pointing out that restrictive provisions were embedded in broadcasting legislation from the inception of the state. He examines the various legal challenges to the Section 31 provision that were made over the years, both in Ireland and in Europe. He concludes that the rationale for Section 31 was characterized by a paternalistic and authoritarian view of the role of the broadcast media. Furthermore, the rationale went beyond a justification based on an immediate threat of violence arising directly from any particular broadcast.

Mark O'Brien locates the enactment of Section 31 legislation within the wider arena of Irish democracy and argues that it was but one of a number of 'silencing projects' at work in Ireland in the 1970s. A siege mentality characterized the body politic of the Republic during this period and manifested itself in four ways: an over-estimation on the part of government that the northern conflict might engulf the southern state, the tacit acceptance of heavy-handed techniques on the part of the Garda Síochána, particularly in security matters, the silencing of the broadcast media and attempts to restrict the print media and the generalised demonisation of alternative viewpoints. The cumulative effect of these processes, O'Brien argues, was to create and perpetuate a climate of fear and silence and to undermine freedom of expression in Irish society.

In Part II, 'Censorship and Journalistic Practice,' the contributors take the reader inside RTÉ and other media institutions, and reflect on how Section 31 impacted on managerial, editorial and journalist practice. As a senior manager in RTÉ during the 1970s, Desmond Fisher had firsthand experience of the often fractious relationship between government and RTÉ. At the heart of this relationship is the question as to whether public service broadcasting is an arm of the government of the day, or whether it shares along with the independent press, the role of public watchdog, exercising the right of the people to information and the right of the media to impart it. Fisher details the correspondence relating to coverage of 'The Troubles' between the RTÉ Authority and the Minister with responsibility for broadcasting in the early 1970s. The sacking of the RTÉ authority and the subsequent re-structuring within RTÉ are documented. Fisher concludes that there are no precise rules that can be devised to regulate the relationship of governments with public service broadcasters.

The chilling effect that Section 31 had on the freedom of choice of journalists working in Irish broadcasting is the subject of Colum Kenny's contribution. Now a media lecturer, Kenny previously worked as a reporter/presenter in RTÉ. He details the lengths to which journalists had to go, to ensure that their stories complied with the restrictive provisions of Section 31. As a consequence, many stories about 'The Troubles' were not covered or were covered only in a partial way. He addresses the question as to why the broadcasting ban met with compliance rather than resistance within the RTÉ organization. Finally, Kenny reflects on the renewed need for professionalism and objectivity on the part of journalists in the post-Section 31 era.

Farrel Corcoran offers an overview of RTÉ's vulnerability to manipulation by the forces of the state. He outlines how RTÉ had to learn, through several bitter experiences, how to handle pressure from government and remain true to the ideals of public service broadcasting. As chairman of the RTÉ Authority from 1995 to 2000, he was at the centre of the post-Section 31 adjustments that took place within RTÉ. He reflects on the challenge of breaking out of the censorious mindset that had become institutionaliaed within the organization over the preceding decades.

Media censorship was a consistent and key feature of the way the Irish and British Governments dealt with 'The Troubles' from the outset of violence in 1970, argues Ed Moloney. He examines the impact of both the British and Irish broadcasting bans, suggesting that alongside formal or legalized censorship, an intangible, but arguably more potent form of self-censorship also thrived. According to Moloney, the principal target of censorship provisions was the IRA and its political wing, Sinn Féin, and it was only when the threat of violence emanating from this quarter subsided that formal censorship ended.

In the final part of the book, 'Media, censorship and the public sphere,' the wider implications of censorship in society are examined. Helen Shaw, now an independent media consultant but formerly director of radio at RTÉ, reflects on how a climate of censorship is generated in conflict situations and the implications of that for the coverage of political stories. Drawing on her own experiences of working under the constraints of Section 31, Shaw places the Irish experience in a comparative international context. She expresses concern about the erosion of the public sphere in the absence of an effective, objective and functioning news media.

Mary P. Corcoran argues that a particular conceptualization of journalists and the media audience they serve underlies attempts by governments to restrict access and coverage in the mass media. Journalists are held to be untrustworthy, and audiences are viewed as suggestible and susceptible to manipulation. Corcoran argues that empirical evidence derived from studies of journalists and audiences challenges such views, suggesting that the relationship between the media, the messenger and the audience is considerably more complex and nuanced than governments allow for.

Finally, Michael D. Higgins reflects on the role of public service broadcasting in an increasingly commercialized media world. He regrets the retreat from the public world, and the submission to the commercial imperative. His opposition to Section 31 when it was first introduced, and his decision to revoke it in 1994, are set in the context of his continuing commitment to the ideals that underlie the public service model of broadcasting. He concludes, that as humans we live by stories, and the principles by which stories are selected, the skill with which they are told, and their resonance in our culture are always and forever, of fundamental democratic concern.

Part I

Censorship and the state

1 / Broadcasting and violence: the case for media restriction[1]

CONOR CRUISE O'BRIEN

Any legislation on broadcasting, even limited amending legislation as at present, necessarily raises very fundamental issues: essentially those of freedom in a democratic state and the limits of such freedom ... The seven basic questions which I would put, and to which I would offer tentative answers for your examination, are the following: Has the democratic state the right to pass repressive legislation? Has it the right to restrict freedom of expression? If so, what limitations should apply to such rights? Should the state have greater rights of restriction in relation to broadcasting than to the press? What limitations should there be on the state's right to intervene in broadcasting? When we speak of freedom in broadcasting, whose freedom do we mean and how is it to be defended? Finally, whatever principles we hold valid in relation to these general questions, are there any special circumstances prevailing in our society in our time which make it necessary or prudent to apply these principles in particular ways?

THE LIMITS TO FREEDOM

As regards the first question, I do not suppose there can be many members of this or any other legislature who hold the doctrine that the state should never engage in any kind of repressive legislation. Most of our laws seek to repress something or other, whether it be abuse of drugs, exposure of workers to unnecessary risks, ill-treatment of children, murder, or other undesirable practices. The reason I raise this question first is that in the form of a pejorative slogan it has very often been launched against the legislation I am seeking to amend and will certainly be launched against some parts of the amending legislation. There are of course weighty arguments against such legislation as I am now introducing, and I shall come to these. But I begin with this particular argument, which is clearly invalid, because I am concerned about the implications of its fairly wide

1 This is an edited version of Conor Cruise O'Brien's 1975 speech that introduced the Broadcasting Authority (Amendment) Act 1976. The Act redefined the provisions of Section 31 (see the chapter by Alex White in this book), required that the ministerial order be placed before the Oireachtas every year for renewal or withdrawal and removed the power of the Minister with responsibility for broadcasting to sack the RTE Authority. For a full text of the speech see *Seanad Éireann Debates* 79 (1975) cols 762-99 or the Oireachtas website.

use, especially among young people. Those who use this slogan suggest that, whenever the liberal and democratic state uses repressive legislation, backed as it has to be by the power to coerce those who will not obey the laws, then it is departing from its own principles. The underlying argument, which has often been used by fascists and communists, but is also used by others, is that the liberal and democratic state, by reason of its own principles, has no right to defend itself, or the citizens who look to it for their defence.

This is of course an invitation to the liberal and democratic state to commit suicide. It may be asked in parenthesis whether ours actually *is* a liberal and democratic state. It is, I would say, as democratic as the most democratic country in the world, and about as liberal as that democracy is prepared to stand. It is less liberal than other western European countries but is undoubtedly growing more liberal than it was. Unfortunately the wish to be liberal, or to demand liberalism from others, is often accompanied by only the vaguest notions of what liberalism is, as the slogans about repressive legislation show ... The simple principle which came to be at the heart of the liberal democratic state was laid down for Athens more than two thousand years ago:

> Neither excess of rule nor anarchy
> That is the mean my townsmen shall observe.[2]

All liberal and democratic states have tried to observe that mean, always differing strongly within themselves as to what particular measures may involve 'excess of rule' and what may lead to 'anarchy', but always accepting that anarchy is to be abhorred and that the state must maintain, and where necessary use, an apparatus of repression. It may be well to distinguish here between what one might call practical work-a-day anarchy and the anarchy of the philosophical anarchists. The latter would be a highly desirable thing, if the assumptions on which it were based were true, or could become true. And of course they may one day come true. It may come about, as a result of technological developments and wiser use of that technology, stabilization of world population, elimination of poverty, vastly improved education and understanding of our own psychology, that aggression, cruelty, greed and exploitation of the weak by the strong will disappear altogether from human behaviour and all people will devote their energies to helping one another rather than winning advantages for themselves. In those conditions, anarchy would be a benign state of affairs and repressive legislation would be unthinkable. Whether humanity as a whole may conceivably be moved in that direction I would not care to guess: the question is related to that of the

2 From the *Oresteia* of Aeschylus.

perfectability of man, and might bring us to the perilous fringes of theology. But we are certainly nowhere near such a Utopian state of affairs now, and this country is not noticeably nearer to it than any other country. In present conditions, human nature and the human situation being as they are, anarchy – that is, the breakdown of the state – simply involves disseminated retail-tyranny: forms of rule unchecked either by civilized tradition or by constitutional or conventional safeguards of any kind. Of that, too, we have experience, but I shall come back to that.

I have encountered, in different parts of Africa at different times, in parts of a great American city, and more recently in parts of Northern Ireland, situations in which the gunman for a time is absolute ruler over a given area, fairly large or very small: where the gunman's mind is the sole legislature and judicature, and his armed hand the executive. In comparison to conditions in these squalid and barbarous little empires, the abuses which prevail in the daylight of the effective jurisdiction of a democratic state, serious as they are in absolute terms, pale into relative insignificance. The democratic state has the duty to defend itself and those whom it represents against such threats and such encroachments, and the duty moreover to do so effectively. It has the duty also to defend and where possible extend the general liberties of the citizens to the maximum extent compatible with the secure survival of that on which both the liberties themselves and the prospect of their growth ultimately depend: that is, the democratic state itself.

There is obviously a tight-rope situation here: the democratic state has to save itself on the one hand from being pushed by fear of anarchy into 'excess of rule' and on the other hand to save itself from falling into anarchy through fear of excess of rule. This is a perennial problem. How the balance is best kept at any time and in any place depends on one's judgment of the circumstances prevailing then and there. I shall come later to the question that concerns us most closely: the application of these principles to our own situation, and the balance most appropriate to our conditions. I imagine that all Senators, or almost all, will agree in general with the answer to that first question: that the democratic state has the right to enact repressive legislation, provided that it represses the right things in the right way, and by means that are adequate but not excessive.

THE POWER OF LANGUAGE

Opinions may well be more divided on the second question: Has the state any right to restrict freedom of expression? It is possible to hold that it is best not to do so at all: that the state should restrain, where necessary, overt and material actions, but should leave purely verbal utterances strictly alone. Language, it is urged, can be a safety valve for feelings which might otherwise find more dangerous expression; debate, using even the most heated forms of argument, has a cleansing power; even the most detestable ideas – the advocacy of genocide for example – should be allowed the widest possible public expression, and then be met by reasoned argument. Obviously, I am presenting here an argument with which I am in agreement. This is undoubtedly an attractive concept, especially to those who have an absolute faith in the force of rational argument, as capable of overcoming appeals to the passions. Those who hold to this view often quote with approval certain well-known lines of John Milton, including the famous 'Let her [truth] and falsehood grapple! Who ever knew truth put to the worse in a free and open encounter?' This and other fine sayings have been adduced to support a doctrine that freedom of expression is an absolute, whose untrammeled exercise will necessarily be beneficial to society and that the state has no right to interfere with it. The weakness of the doctrine is that it tends to assume that all discourse consists of rational argument and to ignore the rather obvious fact, not unfamiliar to us in this country, that a word can lead to a blow.

In wider terms, language can be used to inflict pain and arouse cruelty; to instil fear into one group and arouse hatred in another; it can be used to whip up feelings conducive to pogroms; it can be used to exploit revulsion against one atrocity in order to justify the commission of other atrocities; it can be used to legitimize a sustained campaign of violence, to raise funds for that campaign and to confuse or intimidate those who tend to question or oppose such a campaign. Incidentally Milton, who did not in fact favour absolute freedom to publish with impunity, was well aware of the violence with which words can be charged. 'Books,' he wrote, 'are as lively and as vigorously productive as those fabulous Dragons' teeth: and being sown up and down may chance to spring up armed men.' What was true of the printed word in the seventeenth century is certainly no less true of the words far more widely 'sown up and down' today by broadcasting – an emotional appeal is not capable of being dispelled by rational argument alone. An insult, backed by a threat, is not adequately answered by a syllogism. For these and related reasons all states, even the most liberal, have in fact placed some restraints on freedom of expression and indeed liberal states continue to add new restrictions, notably, and rightly, in the field of racially offensive language. The effectiveness of such restrictions is open to question – as is the effectiveness of laws in general – but the placing of legal curbs on defamation, insults, threats, incitement to violence and racial smears is generally accepted as having on the whole salutary effects, as tending to establish desirable norms of behaviour and as being conducive to the peace of society and the well-being of individuals and families. Words are in fact an integral part of many patterns of action. If this is accepted, the absolute distinction between words and actions is broken down, and words and actions together become part of a pattern of behaviour, which is and should be amenable to law.

If we accept, then, that *some* restrictions may be applied to freedom of expression, we come to our third question: What limitations should apply to such restrictions? A line which one might legitimately seek to draw – though it is very hard in practice – is that which would set apart, as belonging to the sphere of action amenable to law, all forms of play on the emotions, through words and images, in ways likely to arouse fear and hatred, to cause acute distress, or to endanger the lives of citizens, and the security of the state responsible for those lives. All other forms of discourse should be the domain of freedom of expression. Any restriction on freedom of speech should have to be shown to be desirable in the general interest, not just the interest of the government of the day. That is very important. Not merely its formal wording, but its actual working should be exposed to continued scrutiny and to renewed debate, so as to ensure that a restriction accepted for the protection of the citizens is not abused for the exclusive benefit of their rulers. I hope this new legislation may meet these tests. I am certain that it meets them better than the legislative provisions which it replaces.

PROTECTING THE PUBLIC AND THE BROADCASTERS

Coming now more closely to the nub of our discussion here, we consider the fourth question, that of what particular rights the state should legitimately exercise in relation to broadcasting, and in particular what restrictions the state may legitimately require in this sphere. Our democratic state does, for example, exert much greater control over broadcasting than over the press. This arises from the nature of the situation: the fact that the electro-magnetic spectrum, unlike newsprint and ink, is public property and cannot readily be bought and sold in separate consignments and that therefore broadcasting has to be controlled, in some degree at least, by the state on behalf of the community, basically through an inherent monopoly in the allocation of frequencies, combined with responsibility to the people in the matter of how these frequencies were used.

If the state allocates the use of a public asset and if it requires citizens who wish to benefit from use of that asset, to pay for their privilege, then the state, on behalf of the citizens who pay the licence fees and elect the government of the state, has a particular responsibility in relation to broadcasting, and specifically the responsibility to ensure that broadcasting is not used to endanger either the security of the state which licensed it, or the lives of the citizens who pay for it. These considerations are greatly reinforced by the fact that broadcasting, of all the media, both through sounds and images, has by far the most immediate impact on people and situations, has by far the greatest capacity to generate emotion, and that its capacities in these regards have aroused and held the fascinated attention of people interested in promoting and justifying violence, and strongly desirous of access to broadcasting for precisely these ends. Professional broadcasters have themselves publicly noted that, in certain conditions, the mere appearance of a television camera on a street may tend to speed up the action of a riot – the speeding up being clearly aimed at the television camera and through it at television screens throughout the area, the presumed object and probable effect of this being to spread similar patterns of conduct more widely ...

This brings us to the fifth question of what limitations there should be on the state's right to intervene. As in other cases the power to regulate needs itself to be regulated carefully so that the response is not excessive and that broadcasting remains free to cover the flow of news adequately and to discuss current affairs intelligently, probingly, comprehensively and with access to a very wide range of opinion. The difficulties involved here are probably never entirely soluble. Dr Johnson implied as much when he wrote: 'The danger of such unbounded liberty, and the danger of bounding it have produced a problem in the science of government, which human understanding seems hitherto unable to solve.' I hope the Senate will take that durable 'hitherto' as a challenge.

This question of the limitations on the state's right to intervene is closely linked to my sixth question: When we speak of freedom in broadcasting, whose freedom do we mean and how is it to be defended? Some people – quite a few people, indeed – have written and spoken as if implying that freedom of broadcasting meant the freedom of any individual broadcaster to broadcast just what he liked. It is not easy to see how this could be defended; to begin with, the general considerations I have already mentioned apply here too. If an individual broadcaster should take it into his head to engage in hate propaganda against a minority, or a majority for that matter, there ought to be someone there to stop him – at least if we accept the essentials of the foregoing argument. In broadcasting, as in other forms of collective activity – in newspapers, for example – no individual is entirely free to do what he likes; and, as in every valid, creative, collective enterprise, each individual involved in the creative process has a considerable say in what goes on: that is to say, the freedom involved is a collective freedom, under law.

There is no doubt that this kind of freedom would be – and was here for some considerable time – stifled by direct day-to-day governmental control over broadcasting – the system which the late Erskine Childers ended.[3] It could also be damaged by indirect covert governmental pressure, exercised nominally in the

---

3 Erskine Childers was a former Fianna Fáil Minister with responsibility for broadcasting.

public interest, but actually in the interests of a person or persons holding power at a given moment in time. Broadcasters have to be protected from that type of interference, just as the public has to be protected against the possible use of broadcasting in support of violent groups hostile to democracy by the exploitation of emotions, through the use of words and images, in such a way as to promote the objectives of such groups. I believe that, on the whole, the present structures, whereby the Director General is nominated by and responsible to an Authority nominated by the elected government, have tended in general to serve these two purposes – never wholly compatible or wholly attainable – of protecting both the public and the broadcasters. But I believe also that these structures can be improved by defining what might be called the reserve powers retained by the government and parliament as relating to security – and security only – and by doing everything possible to eliminate the danger of covert interference for reasons other than those basic reasons on which I have laid stress here. I believe that the strengthening of the authority and the clarifying of its relation to the state are in fact the best means both of upholding the collective freedom of broadcasting and the principle of responsibility to the state ...

IN DEFENCE OF THE DEMOCRATIC STATE

The final question which I posed and which I would now like to discuss is that of whether any special circumstances prevail in our society in our time, which make it necessary or prudent to apply these principles in particular ways? I think our history, both in the more remote past and recently, has placed us today in a situation where the defence of the democratic state, together with the liberal values and civil rights for all citizens which that kind of state alone sustains, requires a high degree of intelligent vigilance and that such vigilance should be turned on our use of words and images and particularly on the broadcasting of these ... Those who express themselves cynically about democracy ought sometimes to remember that democracy is the only form of government about which it is possible to be cynical in public while continuing to live in safety under its jurisdiction. Commentators insist on the failures of democracy and yet tend to assume the survival of democracy as something to be taken for granted. A strong overt commitment to democracy is less than general: indulgent attitudes to certain of the enemies of democracy are frequent. A free press, whose lifespan can be no longer than that of the democratic state under which it exists and under which alone it can exist, has on the whole turned its critical attention more closely on the faults of that state than on the forces which threaten it. This is right, of course, if the faults are great and the threat is slight. The faults are great no doubt, though less I believe than in any other form of organised state that we know. Is the threat slight?

In our conditions there are forces at work which tend to turn the normal sturdy sulkiness of the democratic citizen into something rather more disturbing. There are, to begin with, the lingering elusive doubts about the legitimacy of the state itself. The actual denial of that legitimacy is now confined to a very small, but significant, minority of the population; but the effects of past denials are much more widespread, partly in the forms of doubts, disengagements and disparagements about state and parliament, and partly in ambivalence towards antidemocratic bodies which arrogate to themselves powers rightly belonging to the democratic state. To speak more plainly: too many people speak and write as if the armed conspiracies known as the IRA, have a legitimate or quasi-legitimate, though usually unspecified, role to play in our society. This permeates the language that is used about them and that language in turn reinforces the peculiar kind of authority which they have held, which has done enormous damage, which may seem perhaps at the moment to be on the verge of decomposing but still requires vigilance, plain speaking and determination in combating it. I know that in certain circles, it is regarded as somewhat 'paranoid' even to refer to armed conspiracies. It would, indeed, be paranoid if these conspiracies did not exist. Unfortunately they do exist: one of them murdered a Member of this House last year, and they continue to murder, maim and intimidate – especially intimidate – people every day in this island.[4] It is paranoid, I agree, to see armed conspiracies where none exists. What word is there for a failure to see armed conspiracies where they *do* exist and are murdering our neighbours? But, of course, it is not really a question of a failure to see them but of an unwillingness to use words that accurately define their nature. We prefer woollier appellations; thus the words 'the Republican movement' are vague, convenient, give no offence to the conspirators, and are in frequent use.

I think it would be fair to say of many – though certainly not of all – of those who write and broadcast in this country that they have fallen over the years into a cautiously propitiatory habit of reference towards armed conspiracies within the Republican family. Members of these conspiracies when apprehended, tried and duly convicted are generally referred to as 'Republican prisoners', as if they had been jailed for their opinions and not for their crimes, up to and including murder. Their more spectacular crimes are, indeed, strongly condemned and the armed conspirators are frequently implored to desist from violence. Such condemnations and such pleas are very often mingled with tributes to various virtues imputed to the conspirators, and a generous attribution of space to all their com-

---

4 The killing by the IRA of Fine Gael Senator Billy Fox in March 1974.

muniqués and all the hand-outs of the numerous associations whose only significance derives from the consistency of their alignment with the position of one or other wing of the IRA. There is also a disquieting tendency to attach credence, or the appearance of credence, to statements by the propaganda wings of these conspiracies, in spite of the fact that they have lied, and been caught lying, on so many occasions. I would attach only symptomatic importance here to various individual phrases. One could compile a long list of them; I will mention just a few – the use in a newspaper of the word 'execution' to describe an IRA murder; the uttering by a columnist of a 'shout of joy' at the news of the Portlaoise escapes; the placing by a Dublin periodical very recently of inverted commas round the word 'convicted' in relation to a convicted criminal of Republican tendencies; the use by a commentator of the phrase 'subversive organizations, as the government calls them'. None of these items is of much significance in itself: what is significant is the frequency with which language of this kind is used, the ease with which it is accepted, and the widespread equivocal approach to the IRA in our society which this implies. It is rather rare to find any explicit total rejection of the IRA as having any legitimate role in our society; any explicit recognition of the fact that, in a democracy, there is room for only one army, the army responsible to the people through an elected government and that the citizens should co-operate with the government in breaking any private army ...

RESISTING THE CULT OF VIOLENCE

I believe that our public are now clear sighted enough about the IRA, that they see its danger generally, detect the falsity of its promises and want nothing to do with it. The IRA's senseless destructive campaign in Northern Ireland has accomplished that much at least. But a certain miasma of glamour about these organizations still lingers in the channels of communications. This is not entirely due to the way in which explicit communications tend to lag behind the intuitive processes through which ordinary citizens reach their conclusions. There are also, as in the question of attitudes to democracy, factors of more widespread application, not confined to our island. Just as violence is attracted to the camera, so the camera is attracted to violence; it is a case of love at first sight on both sides. This is, of course, due not just to the perversity of cameramen or broadcasters generally, but to the fascination which violence has for so many people – especially for people who can witness or hear about it happening to others from the safety of their own living-room. The fascination too may have diminished for viewers in the Republic, as the violence has come nearer. The news value of violence in itself confers an authority of a kind on those who can dispense violence and even on those more remotely connected with it. The utterances of Sinn Féin would certainly not attract one-fifth the attention they do if their spokesmen were not rightly felt to be speaking for the gunmen, in spite of their ritual denials that this is so. These sympathies, these half-sympathies, these equivocations have their roots in history. This is true, but it is not a reason for not trying to eliminate them – as many European nations who also have a history, have eliminated their equivalents – if we now find them to be noxious to our own lives and those of our children.

Many people who originally cherished such sympathies have already weighed them and found them altogether wanting, as far as our life now is concerned. Others, perhaps, while not really supporting the armed conspiracies, would concede them a sort of privileged role, sanctified by historic precedent, existing on a plane above normal judgment and enjoying, if not a legal immunity, a kind of moral immunity for acts which, if committed by ordinary citizens, would be crimes. This attitude, understandable enough perhaps in the 1920s and 1930s, seems now, in 1975, surely to have something sickly and retarded about it. In any case the state has to reject firmly any such concept of historically privileged crime, and this rejection will necessarily be reflected in legislation and regulations affecting the state broadcasting system. This is not because there is any serious danger at the present time that material sympathetic to the IRA would cause the citizens of the Republic to engage in widespread violence. The results, the dangers are more long-term, and therefore all the more appropriate to be guarded against by legislation. Basically, if the state broadcasting system were in any way to accredit the idea that the IRA is a quasi-legitimate institution or that it is appropriate for citizens to be neutral as between the democratic state and the armed conspiracies which seek to usurp its functions – and have on occasions actually usurped some of them – then that pattern of presentation coming from that source – that is, a source closely associated with the state itself – would tend to confuse the citizens, by intensifying the false air of legitimacy with which the IRA has managed to surround itself and would thereby under any propitious conditions which might occur and there might be such conditions, further the criminal purposes of that organization.

Of no less importance than this is consideration of the impact of our broadcasting in Northern Ireland – and, of course, our sound broadcasting can reach virtually all of Northern Ireland and our television some 14 or 15 per cent of viewers there – where there exists among the majority a widespread impression – greatly, understandably and most ominously strengthened by certain events of five years ago – that this state is in some kind of collusion with the IRA.[5] Anything in our broadcasting that would seem to confirm that false impression is

5 The Arms Crisis of 1970.

directly dangerous to life, both in Northern Ireland and here, and I think Senators will know that I do not exaggerate there. In normal circumstances, and I hope in all circumstances likely to arise, it is for the broadcasting authority itself to ensure that a proper balance is kept, through the discharge of its responsibilities under law. But in view of the serious implications of these matters for the state and its people, it is necessary for the state to retain a reserve power of intervention which may never be used, but is there in case of need ...

I am not under the illusion that any restrictive provisions embodied in broadcasting legislation can be one hundred per cent effective. The 1960 Act, which in its present form is considerably more sweeping and drastic in its provisions than it will be if these amendments are carried, was yet by no means always successful in restraining the kind of manifestations which it was presumably intended to restrain. Legislation is static; broadcasting fluid and volatile; broadcasters always impatient of curbs and on occasions ingenious in evading them. Restraints work only in a clumsy, intermittent and painful fashion unless those concerned are themselves convinced of a *need* for some restraints. If of course it were certain that all broadcasters were convinced of such a need and would in all circumstances remain so, then there would be no need for any external legislative restraint. However, this is not likely to be the case. The broadcaster's professional instinct, I believe, inclines him or her towards exposure of what is exciting, even sensational and to regard the possible social effects of such exposure as conjectural and outside his or her sphere. Instances of active sympathy with the armed conspiracies and desire to promote their cause by propaganda are rare, though not altogether unknown. A kind of neutral professionalism, indifferent to social consequences, is much more widespread and lasting. It is for this reason that the public interest has, in the government's view, to be protected ...

2 / Section 31: ministerial orders and court challenges

ALEX WHITE

The broadcasting ban known as 'Section 31' in fact was a ministerial order made *under* Section 31 of the Broadcasting Authority Acts 1960–1976. The Section itself came into being in 1960 and was repealed, finally, some forty years later in 2001. The first order under Section 31 was made in 1971 by the then Minister for Post and Telegraphs, Gerard Collins. The last annual order was made in 1993, so the ban could be said to have ended in 1994 when it was not renewed by the then Minister for Arts, Culture and the Gaeltacht, Michael D. Higgins.[1] Section 31 (1) of the Broadcasting Authority Act, 1960 provided that: 'The Minister may direct the [RTE] Authority in writing to refrain from broadcasting any particular matter of any particular class and the Authority shall comply with the direction.'

This was the original enabling provision. Clearly it had no force unless the Minister *actually directed* the Authority 'to refrain from broadcasting' any particular material, and this was done for the first time in 1971. A number of amendments to the 1960 Act were introduced in 1976[2] including a new and narrower formulation for Section 31.[3] Thereafter, the orders under Section 31 could be made for one year only at a time. There was also a new requirement that the orders should in future be placed before the Oireachtas[4], thus allowing for at least some measure of parliamentary scrutiny, though in practice there was very little debate or discussion concerning the measure in the ensuing years.

In the course of the forty years or so during which Section 31 was on the statute books, and the twenty-three years of its actual operation, the broadcasting ban was considered by the courts on little more than half a dozen occasions. There was one major (unsuccessful) constitutional challenge, the *Lynch*[5] case in 1982. There was also an application to the European Commission of Human Rights under the European Convention, the *Purcell*[6] case, which was rejected in 1991. Apart from this, towards the very end of the period of operation of the ban, there were a small number of challenges to the method of application of the orders by RTÉ and the independent radio and television stations.[7]

---

1 See the chapter by Michael D. Higgins, below.   2 By way of the Broadcasting Authority (Amendment) Act 1976.   3 See below.   4 As opposed to the government, as previously had been the position.   5 *The State (Lynch) v. Cooney* [1982] IR 337, 361.   6 *Purcell and Others v. Ireland* [1991] 12 HRLJ 254, 260.   7 The *O'Toole* and *Brandon Books* cases. See below.

HISTORICAL CONTEXT

A radio service had been established in 1926 but until the mid-1950s there was virtually no political broadcasting apart from news bulletins. The fact that Radio Éireann essentially was a branch of the Department of Posts and Telegraphs and its employees were civil servants, ensured a high level of control of the station by the government. Apart from party political broadcasts[8] elected politicians were not even permitted to take part in radio programmes, and even after the introduction of current affairs programmes in 1953, 'the greatest care was taken to avoid topics and material that were at all likely to evoke even a whiff of party controversy and, if possible, any controversy at all'.[9]

With the commencement of domestic television in Ireland, the government moved to establish a legislative framework for broadcasting incorporating both radio and television. This was done by way of the Broadcasting Authority Act 1960, which established Radio Telefís Éireann on a statutory basis under an Authority to be appointed by the government. When the Act was being considered by the Oireachtas, there would appear to have been little if any debate on the powers contained at Section 31. The Minister for Posts and Telegraphs, Michael Hilliard, spoke in the Seanad of the possible use of Section 31 'to prevent the broadcast of morally objectionable programmes'.[10] The Minister went on to express the hope that it would not be necessary to invoke the power given in the Section at all.

In any event, there was little discussion of the measure as a form of political censorship, nor even (as was the primary focus a decade later) as an instrument of state security, despite the fact that the IRA had been active in a border campaign throughout the 1950s and into the early 1960s.[11] That there should have been such relative indifference to the provision or its likely effects may not be very surprising, given that radio broadcasting in Ireland had no particular history of robust independence in its political coverage, and domestically produced television was an entirely new development at that stage. In any event, it seems clear that at least one aspect of the government's thinking was that it should reserve a power to impose a form of political censorship should the occasion, in its view, require it. As Minister Hilliard stated in the Dáil: 'There must be reserved to the Government some means of ultimate control over broadcasts which might be inimical to the national interest.'[12]

---

8 Introduced in 1954. 9 Chubb, B. (1974) *The government and politics of Ireland.* Oxford: Oxford University Press, 134. Chubb described Radio Éireann in the pre-1960s era as 'truly a political eunuch'. 10 *Seanad Éireann Debates* 52 (1960) cols 5–23. 11 One of a small number of critics was Senator Owen Sheehy Skeffington who said that the Section was 'unnecessary and potentially dangerous' as it gave the Minister a complete veto over every item and class of item without reference to the RTÉ Authority. *Seanad Éireann Debates* 52 (1960) cols 528–41 cited in Hall, W. (1993) *The electronic age.* Dublin: Oak Tree Press, 226. 12 *Dáil Éireann Debates* 179 (1960) cols 761.

But while political broadcasting and current affairs coverage gradually became more confident and hard-hitting in the 1960s, it was not until the outbreak of the 'Northern Troubles' at the very end of the decade and, perhaps most decisively, the resultant trauma within the Southern state in 1970 and 1971, that the government invoked Section 31 and imposed the broadcasting ban. That the government did not see any *need* for a broadcasting ban in the 1960s seems to be the only credible explanation for the absence of such a measure. Certainly, such absence cannot be attributed to a principled view on the part of the government that RTÉ should be independent in its coverage of current affairs.[13]

INTRODUCTION OF THE BROADCASTING BAN IN 1971

The civil rights movement emerged in the North in 1968 and 1969 and over the following years the modern 'Troubles' ignited. The IRA, which had been dormant since the end of the border campaign in 1962, again became active. There was a marked intensification of violent conflict on the streets of the North, characterized by what many commentators saw as a particularly brutal response on the part of the northern police force and the 'B Specials'. Combined with these developments was a greater availability and penetration of broadcast media, especially television. As a result of this, the 'Northern Troubles' became a world television event contributing to a heightened sense of crisis in the Southern state as well as in the North.

The sense of an internal threat to the state and its institutions by the Provisional IRA was frequently underscored in public statements by government ministers of the time. Indeed, one year prior to the imposition of the first order, the Minister for Justice, Desmond O'Malley, in a letter to his colleague, the Minister for Posts and Telegraphs, had complained about certain individuals being allowed to appear on television who were openly identified as members of the IRA: 'When is this going to stop? Is the RTÉ Authority going to sit back and allow the television and radio stations to be used by this minority to brainwash the public?'[14]

This formed the context in which the Section 31 orders were introduced from 1971. Thus O'Malley explained the basis for the Section 31 order as being: 'To discourage recruitment to subversive organizations dedicated to the use of force'.[15] The first order was made following a *Seven Days* programme on RTÉ television in September 1971, which included interviews with members of the IRA, an illegal organization. The order directed RTÉ:

---

13 See the chapter by Farrel Corcoran, below.   14 Hall, W., op. cit., 234.   15 See Hogan, 'The demise of the Irish broadcasting ban' (1994) 1 EPL 69.

> To refrain from broadcasting any matter of the following class i.e. any
> matter that could be calculated to promote the aims and activities of any
> organization which engages in, promotes, encourages or advocates the
> attaining of any particular objective by violent means.

Dr Conor Cruise O'Brien, then a Labour Party opposition spokesman (and later
a staunch advocate of the measure),[16] criticized the initial ministerial order in tren-
chant terms. He argued that radio and television had become 'less free in relation
to the state' because of the directive issued by the Minister under Section 31.[17]

THE BROADCASTING AUTHORITY (AMENDMENT) ACT 1976

A new government came into office in March 1973. Dr Conor Cruise O'Brien,
who was appointed Minister for Posts and Telegraphs, made an order under the
then existing Section 31, but subsequently went on to introduce the Amendment
Act of 1976, which included a new formulation for Section 31. The terms of the
new Section were somewhat narrower than the 1960 version, and confined the
ministerial ban to circumstances where s/he was:

> of the opinion that the broadcasting of a particular matter or any matter
> of a particular class would be likely to promote, or incite to, crime or
> would tend to undermine the authority of the State, he may, by order,
> direct the Authority[18] to refrain from broadcasting the matter or any mat-
> ter of the particular class, and the Authority shall comply with the order.[19]

In the course of the Seanad debate on the 1976 Amendment Act, the Minister
stated:

> Basically, if the State broadcasting system were in any way to accredit the
> idea that the IRA is a quasi legitimate institution, or that it is appropriate
> for citizens to be neutral as between the democratic state and the armed

16 See the chapter by Conor Cruise O'Brien, above. 17 See Hall, W., op. cit., 235ff. Hall recalls that a year later, in
November 1972, Dr Garret Fitzgerald also criticized the Minister for Posts and Telegraphs regarding the concept of
the 'national interest' in the context of the Section 31 directive saying: '[Y]ou could not allow a Government of one
party in Parliament to have the undisputed power to determine that something should not be broadcast in the national interest. There is something inherently unbalanced about the idea of a Government deciding what is in the national interest. The Government can decide what is in the Government's interest. They can have a view of what is in the
national interest. You cannot legally define the national interest as what the Government want. To do so would be to
destroy democracy complete': *Dáil Éireann Debates* 263 (1972) col. 2460. Hall notes that Dr Fitzgerald argued that the
power to issue a directive should be constrained by the necessity to have the directive countersigned by the leader of
one of the opposition parties. 18 The RTÉ Authority. An identical provision was introduced covering the independent sector in the Radio and Television Act 1988. 19 Section 16, Broadcasting Authority (Amendment) Act 1976.

conspiracies which seek to usurp its functions – and have on occasions actually usurped some of them – then that pattern of presentation coming from that source – that is, a source closely associated with the State itself – would tend to confuse the citizens, by intensifying the false air of legitimacy with which the IRA has managed to surround itself and would thereby under any propitious conditions which might occur, and there might be such conditions, further the criminal purposes of that organization.[20]

The justification for the Section 31 orders appears to have drawn heavily on a particular view of the power of broadcasting, to the extent that the government believed that the very appearance on radio or television of a spokesman (and in practice a 'spokesman' included any member) would tend to 'glamourize' that person and, by extension, the organization of which he or she was a member. The reference to views which it was 'appropriate for citizens' to have and also to matters which 'would tend to confuse the citizens' certainly reflected a remarkably paternalistic and authoritarian view, both of the role and function of broadcasting and of the reasoning powers of the average citizen.

Under the terms of the Amendment Act, an order under Section 31 was to remain in force for a maximum of twelve months, but could be extended by further orders of similar duration. Although the law provided for the annulment of the ban by either House of the Oireachtas, this never in fact occurred. Indeed, as previously mentioned, there was virtually no parliamentary discussion or debate concerning Section 31 throughout the entire period of its operation. Typically, a new order would be laid before the Oireachtas at or about the time of the expiry of the previous order and this occurred with predictable regularity until 1994, irrespective of which parties were in government.[21] The orders were essentially identical in format and content from year to year, though from time to time new organizations were added to the list of groups banned from the airwaves.

---

20 See the chapter by Conor Cruise O'Brien, above. The language here is perhaps reminiscent of a Ministerial speech to the Seanad some thirty-five years earlier, in a debate on newspapers censorship during the Second World War. On that occasion Mr Frank Aiken, Minister for External (later Foreign) Affairs, stated: 'It is no change to the ordinary people of the country to have myself and my staff acting as Censor. It is only a change of function from the Editor of the Irish Times to myself and my staff. It is we who have the final OK on what to cut out instead of the editors and in certain circumstances, when this country is in such grave danger as it is at the moment, I think the people are better pleased that the censorship should be in the hands of somebody who is responsible to the parliament elected by the people rather than of persons who are appointed by boards of directors and have no responsibility to the people, though normally they act in a decent way towards them': *Seanad Éireann Debates* 24 (1940) col. 2610.   21 The only exception was in January 1986 when the two Sinn Féin the Workers' Party TDs put down a Dáil motion seeking to prevent the renewal of the ban. However, the motion did not obtain the required minimum number of Deputies (7) required in order to force a debate.

Perhaps the most striking, and certainly the most controversial aspect of the ministerial orders made under Section 31 was that they were applied, in practice, to *individuals* and not to particular *speech*. That this should be so is scarcely apparent from a reading of the text of the orders that referred to 'spokesmen', suggesting that such persons were banned when they were actually acting as spokesmen for any one of the named organizations, or when they were 'representing, or purporting to represent' the particular groups involved. However, as we shall see, the interpretation placed upon the terms of the order, in particular by RTÉ, was to exclude *any member* of such groups or organizations, irrespective of the subject matter of their broadcast.[22]

SECTION 31 IN THE COURTS: CONSTITUTIONAL CHALLENGE

The courts have an important role in reviewing the exercise of executive power by the government and by ministers. This can sometimes involve the courts in an analysis of a particular ministerial measure, the statutory basis or authority for such ministerial order, and the legality of the exercise of the particular power - most especially in the context of the provisions of the Constitution. In February 1982 the Minister for Posts and Telegraphs made a Section 31 order directing RTÉ to refrain from carrying any broadcast by or on behalf of Provisional Sinn Féin. The order was to prevent party political broadcasts on behalf of Sinn Féin that RTÉ had agreed to broadcast. Sean Lynch, one of the seven Sinn Féin candidates in the general election of February 1982, then brought a constitutional challenge to the order and to Section 31 itself. Article 40, Section 6, sub-section 1 of the Irish Constitution provides as follows:

> The State guarantees liberty for the exercise of the following rights, subject to public order and morality:
>
>> The right of the citizens to express freely their convictions and opinions.
>>
>> The education of public opinion being, however, a matter of such grave import to the common good, the State shall endeavour to ensure that organs of public opinion, such as the radio, the press, the cinema, while preserving their rightful liberty of expression, including criticism of Government policy, shall not be used to undermine public order or morality or the authority of the State.

---

22 This remained the position until the 1993 Supreme Court judgment in the *O'Toole* case, delivered within the final year of operation of the Section 31 orders. See below.

It has been suggested that this particular formulation of freedom of expression is very tentative in nature, to the extent that the freedom could be said to be 'conceded rather than declared'.[23] Nevertheless, the Irish Constitution does contain this important, if heavily qualified, guarantee of freedom of expression. The question arising from Mr Lynch's challenge, therefore, was whether Section 31 of the Broadcasting Act and the orders made thereunder were permissible in the context of this constitutional guarantee.

Mr Lynch succeeded in the High Court, where Mr Justice O'Hanlon found that the provisions of Section 31 gave the Minister excessive powers and were therefore unconstitutional. The state appealed this decision to the Supreme Court, which found the Section to be constitutional and held that evidence given to the court regarding the aims, methods and organization of Sinn Féin fully justified the Minister's opinion as to the necessity for the ban. The then Chief Justice concluded as follows:

> The basis for any attempt at control [of freedom of expression and free speech] must be, according to the Constitution, the overriding considerations of public order and public morality. The constitutional provision in question refers to organs of public opinion and these must be held to include the television as well as radio. It places upon the State the obligation to ensure that these organs of public opinion shall not be used to undermine public order or public morality or the authority of the State. It follows that the use of such organs of opinion for the purpose of securing or advocating support for organizations which seek by violence to overthrow the State or its institutions is a use which is prohibited by the Constitution. Therefore, it is clearly the duty of the State to intervene to prevent broadcasts on radio or television which are aimed at such a result, or which in any way would be likely to have the effect of promoting or inciting to crime or endangering the authority of the State. These, however, are objective determinations and obviously the fundamental rights of citizens to express freely their convictions and opinions cannot be curtailed or prevented on any irrational or capricious ground. It must be presumed that when the Oireachtas conferred these powers on the Minister, it intended that they be exercised only in conformity with the Constitution.[24]

In the *Lynch* case, the High Court found that Section 31 offended against the Irish Constitution since the scope of the Minister's power was too wide. The Supreme Court reversed this finding and said that the power was not too wide and that it

---

23 McGonagle, M. (2002) *Media Law*. Dublin: Thompson Round Hall, 337.   24 *The State (Lynch) v. Cooney* [1982] IR 337, 361.

was capable of review on the grounds of reasonableness. However, the Supreme Court went further, and essentially found that, so long as the Minister was satisfied as to the need for an order, it was not for the courts to question the basis for that opinion. This failure on the part of the Supreme Court to scrutinize the grounds for the Minister's decision may be open to criticism.[25] And while the judgment did not of itself change the existing legal position, it had significant consequences by removing any suggestion that Section 31, or the orders, could be challenged on constitutional grounds.

Indeed, the Supreme Court judgment in the *Lynch* case was frequently pointed to as not just a confirmation of the constitutionality of Section 31, but as a 'green light to continue the ban'.[26] It is noteworthy that the Chief Justice referred to 'the duty of the State' to prevent broadcasts aimed at the overthrow of the state by violence. So, not only was the Minister entitled to make the order which he did, he had a 'duty' to do so. One could hardly conceive of a more unequivocal judicial endorsement of the Section 31 orders. Whatever doubt there may have been as to the scope of the orders prior to the *Lynch* case, RTÉ now proceeded on the basis that the ministerial ban affected any member of the organizations listed in the order. This was irrespective of the subject matter of any proposed broadcast. Ironically, therefore, a court action in pursuit of freedom of expression had the opposite result, fortifying the restrictions contained in the broadcasting ban.

SECTION 31 IN EUROPE

In the course of the decade or so following the judgment in the *Lynch* case, the courts were again called upon to consider aspects of the Section 31 orders, and in particular the question of the scope of the orders. In addition, there was an important challenge to the broadcasting ban at the European Commission of Human Rights. In 1989 a group of eighteen journalists and producers in RTÉ, together with their trade unions, SIPTU and the NUJ, lodged an application with the European Commission of Human Rights.[27] The application, *Purcell & Others v. Ireland*,[28] contended that the Section 31 orders were in breach of Article 10 of the European Convention on Human Rights which provides:

25 See discussion by Eoin O'Dell, lecturer in Law, Trinity College Dublin in his paper 'The sound of silence – political dissent and the Broadcasting Ban' delivered at a Symposium on Freedom of Expression at TCD, 6 December 2003. 26 See McGonagle, M., op. cit., 345. Perhaps the most notorious example of the rigidity of RTÉ's position in this period was the station's dismissal of journalist Jenny McGeever in 1988. A report, which Ms McGeever had prepared for the *Morning Ireland* programme on the funeral of three alleged IRA members killed in Gibraltar contained a few words from Martin McGuinness of Sinn Féin. 27 The Commission was a screening mechanism for the Court. It was subsequently abolished and now all applications to the European Court of Human Rights go directly to the Court, though there remains an internal screening process. 28 ECmHR, Decision of 16 April 1991,

1. Everyone has the right to freedom of expression. This right shall include freedom to hold opinions and to receive and impart information and ideas without interference by public authority and regardless of frontiers. This Article shall not prevent States from requiring the licensing of broadcasting, television or cinema enterprises.

2. The exercise of these freedoms, since it carries with it duties and responsibilities, may be subject to such formalities, conditions, restrictions or penalties as are prescribed by law and are necessary in a democratic society, in the interests of national security, territorial integrity or public safety, for the prevention of disorder or crime, for the protection of health or morals, for the protection of the reputation or rights of others, for preventing the disclosure of information received in confidence, or for maintaining the authority and impartiality of the judiciary.

The *Purcell* applicants argued that the Section 31 orders were in breach of the Article 10 freedoms. In reply, the Irish government justified the orders under Section 31 in the context of the ongoing security situation in both parts of Ireland and in Britain. A detailed account of the activities of the Provisional IRA and of the other paramilitary groups listed in the ministerial orders was furnished to the Commission. As to the scope of the order, it was contended by the Irish government that it was necessary to prohibit broadcasts irrespective of the subject matter of such broadcasts.

In its decision rejecting the *Purcell* application, the Commission appeared to accept the argument that the broadcast media had an especially powerful impact and that accordingly, the very *appearance* of a spokesman on radio or television (i.e. irrespective of what he or she was saying) would accord that person a certain enhanced legitimacy. Therefore, the Commission concluded the Section 31 restriction could be deemed to be necessary to democracy under the terms of Article 10 (2). In any event, the application to the European Commission on Human Rights was rejected and in this regard it may be useful to set out the essential elements of the Commission's decision:

> the defeat of terrorism is a public interest of the first importance in a democratic society. In a situation where politically motivated violence poses a constant threat to the lives and security of the population, and where the advocates of this violence seek access to the mass media for publicity purposes, it is particularly difficult to strike a fair balance between the requirements of protecting freedom of information and the imperatives of protecting the State and the public against armed conspiracies seeking to overthrow the democratic order which guarantees this freedom and other human rights.

Called upon to consider whether the Section 31 order can be said to strike this balance in conformity with the provisions of Article 10 (2) ... the Commission notes that the restrictions resulting from the order do not refer to the contents of radio and television programmes... rather, they are designed to deny representatives of known terrorist organizations and their political supporters the possibility of using the broadcast media as a platform for advocating their cause, encouraging support for their organizations and conveying the impression of legitimacy.

The Commission recognises that some of these restrictions, particularly the ban on live interviews with spokesmen of the listed organizations, may cause the Applicants inconvenience in the exercise of their professional duties, but it does not, on balance, find that they amount to restrictions on the Applicant's right to freedom of expression, which are incompatible with ... Article 10 ...

In contemporary society, radio and television are media of considerable power and influence. Their impact is more immediate than that of the print media, and the possibilities for the broadcaster to correct, qualify, interpret or comment on any statement made on radio or television are limited in comparison with those available to journalists within the press. Live statements could also involve a special risk of coded messages being conveyed, a risk, which even conscientious journalists cannot control within the exercise of their professional judgment.

Given the limited scope of the restrictions imposed on the Applicants and the overriding interests they were designed to protect, the Commission finds that they can reasonably be considered 'necessary in a democratic society' within the meaning of Article 10 (2)... [29]

In its emphasis on the objective of defeating terrorism, the Commission essentially indicated that this objective outweighed any concerns that may have existed regarding freedom of expression.

BACK TO COURT: O'TOOLE AND BRANDON BOOKS

While the prospects for further challenges to the broadcasting ban looked hopeless following *Lynch* and *Purcell*, there remained one 'loose end'. This related to the restrictive manner in which the ban was actually applied, notably by RTÉ.[30] Even

---

(1991) 12 HRLJ 254. It should be noted that the author was one of the Applicants in this case, along with Ms Purcell and 16 other RTÉ journalists and producers.   29 (1991) 12 HRLJ 254, 260.   30 The first licences for independent broadcasters were not granted until after the passing of the Radio and Television Act, 1988. In any event, RTÉ remained the leading 'player' in the context of the operation of the ban and the independent sector seemed unlikely at that stage to take a different approach to that of RTÉ.

in the *Lynch* judgment, there was no authority for RTÉ's rigid approach in excluding any *member* irrespective of subject matter. On the contrary, Mr Justice Walsh
had stated in that case that Section 31 contained:

> no prohibition against the prosecutor [Mr Lynch] broadcasting on behalf
> of his own candidature. However, any broadcast he might make which
> would represent or promote the views or objects of his political party was
> prohibited'.[31]

Remarkably, however, RTÉ persisted in its policy of excluding any member of
any of the listed organizations irrespective of content or subject matter. Was this
an over-application of the terms of the order? It was perhaps inevitable that this
question would come before the courts, though it did so rather late in the lifetime of the Section 31 ban to have any practical effect.

In 1990, the chairman of a strike committee at the Gateaux bakery in Dublin,
Larry O'Toole, was banned from being interviewed on RTÉ about the dispute.
This was successfully challenged by Mr O'Toole in the High Court where Mr
Justice O'Hanlon found that RTÉ was wrong in its interpretation of the ministerial order invoking Section 31 and held that RTÉ had misinterpreted the order
by applying it to ordinary members of Sinn Féin, when it was clearly confined to
representatives of, and spokespersons for, Sinn Féin.[32]

The Supreme Court upheld the judgment of Mr Justice O'Hanlon, confirm-
ing that the Section 31 order only applied to spokespersons for, and representatives of, Sinn Féin, and not to ordinary members speaking on an innocuous subject, who 'should be treated equally with others when [their] views do not trans-
gress either the Constitution or the law'.[33] Chief Justice Finlay held in the same
case that 'a ban on the broadcasting on any subject or under any circumstances
by a person who is a member of Sinn Féin, cannot … be justified as an implementation of the order'.[34]

Soon after the *O'Toole* case, a further challenge was made to a ban by RTÉ on
an advertisement promoting a book of short stories written by Gerry Adams,
president of Sinn Féin.[35] The advertisement consisted of a voice piece by Mr
Adams himself, though with no political content as such. RTÉ stated that it
would only broadcast the advertisement if it were voiced by a member of Irish
Actors Equity who would not be precluded by Section 31. On the basis that Gerry
Adams was the public face of Sinn Féin,[36] according to RTÉ to allow him to
broadcast on any subject 'no matter how innocuous, would, in fact, amount to

---

31 [1982] IR 337, 368. 32 *O'Toole v. RTÉ*, Unreported, High Court, 31 July 1992. 33 *O'Toole v. RTÉ*, [1993] ILRM 454,
467 *per* Mr Justice O'Flaherty. 34 Ibid., 464–5. 35 'The Street and Other Stories'. 36 Or 'Mr Sinn Féin' as Dr
Conor Cruise O'Brien described him in the course of his [Cruise O'Brien's] court evidence in support of RTÉ.

inviting support for Sinn Féin, [and] be in fact a broadcast by a person representing Sinn Féin and tend to undermine the authority of the State'.[37]

In the High Court, Mr Justice Carney held that whether this was the case was a matter of judgment for RTÉ, and that it was not appropriate for the court to intervene. In a challenge to a similar ban by the IRTC[38] on the same advertisement, Mr Justice Carney accepted that there was evidence to support the IRTC's view that 'Mr Adams could not be separated from his office as President of Sinn Féin and that any broadcast by him on any topic would have the de facto effect of advocating support for Sinn Féin'.[39]

The *O'Toole* judgment had invalidated what effectively had been an over-application of the remit of the Section 31 orders by RTÉ. The judgment in *Brandon Books*, though it rejected the challenge to the ban in that instance, came only three months prior to the date when the Minister would have to decide on the question of renewing the ban for a further year. In that respect, the focus moved from the courts back to the government and the Oireachtas. The Minister, Michael D. Higgins, became the first Minister not to renew the ban in January 1994. Ultimately, some seven years later in 2001, Section 31 itself was repealed.[40]

CONCLUSION

The forty-year period during which Section 31 was on the statute books may perhaps best be considered in four distinct phases:

- Phase I (1960–1971), when the Section lay dormant;
- Phase II (1971–1976) when orders were made under the 1960 Act;
- Phase III (1976–1994) when annual orders were made under the amended version of Section 31, and a number of largely unsuccessful legal challenges were launched in the domestic and European courts; and
- Phase IV (1994–2001) when, as in Phase I, the amended Section remained on the statute books but was not invoked.

There can be little doubt that the rationale for the use of Section 31 was characterized by a paternalistic and authoritarian view of the role of the broadcast media. Ministerial references to views that were 'appropriate for citizens' to hold, and to the risk that the same citizens might otherwise become 'confused' were it

---

37 *Brandon Book Publishers v. RTÉ* [1993] ILRM 806.   38 Independent Radio and Television Commission (now the Broadcasting Commission of Ireland).   39 *Brandon Book Publishers v. IRTC*, Unreported, High Court, 29 October 1993.   40 By way of the Broadcasting Act 2001, First Schedule.

not for the ban, lay at the heart of the justification for the use of Section 31.[41]
This rationale went beyond a justification based on an immediate threat of violence or other adverse consequence arising directly from any particular broadcast.

In this regard, it is important to note that even if the government had never
invoked Section 31, there was in existence throughout the entire period an entirely separate statutory provision banning material that 'may reasonably be regarded
as being likely to promote, or incite to, crime or as tending to undermine the
authority of the State'.[42] It must be assumed that the various ministers did not
regard this provision as sufficient for their purpose. Instead of relying on this
restriction in Section 18, it was felt necessary to have a more explicit directive
under Section 31.

We have seen that the justification for the ban was the need, as the government
saw it, to prevent the airwaves being used to 'glamorize', or to confer legitimacy
on certain individuals. It may be that the government believed – undoubtedly
correctly – that Section 18 could not be extended to a general prohibition on
individuals (or spokesmen), other than in circumstances where they were, say,
advocating violence or crime.

It has been argued, notably in a long line of cases from the United States
Supreme Court, that the proper test for any restrictions on freedom of expression, including freedom of the press, is whether the speech or material concerned
is used in such circumstances and is of such a nature as to create 'a clear and present danger that [it] will bring about…substantive evils…'[43] In the context of a
broadcasting ban, this 'clear and present danger' test requires a high level of immi-
nent risk that words spoken on radio or television will lead to some form of danger or 'evil'. It cannot be a generalised or vague risk of something occurring in
the future; it must be a risk of harm essentially resulting immediately from the
broadcast.[44] In contrast, Section 31 referred to material that would be 'likely' to
promote, or incite to crime or would 'tend' to undermine the authority of the
state. This formulation – upheld, as we have seen by the Supreme Court in *The
State (Lynch) v. Cooney*[45] – could not remotely be said to conform to a 'clear and present danger' test. Rather, it would appear to allow for a wide measure of latitude
in the determination of what might be 'likely' to promote or incite to crime, or
'tend' to undermine the authority of the state.

---

41 See n37.   42 Section 18(1)(A) of the Broadcasting Authority Act 1960 as inserted by the 1976 Amendment Act.
43 *Per* Holmes J in *Schenck v. US*, 249 US 47 (1919).   44 In *Whitney v. California*, 274 US 357 (1927) Brandeis J delivered a famous dissenting judgment (along with Holmes J), which later became the accepted reasoning to be applied
to restrictions on freedom of expression: 'There must be reasonable ground to believe that the evil to be prevented
is a serious one … even advocacy of violation, however reprehensible morally, is not a justification for denying free
speech where the advocacy falls short of incitement and there is nothing to indicate that the advocacy would be
immediately acted on.'   45 [1982] IR 337.

In this regard, one commentator, Eoin O'Dell, has observed that 'neither a likelihood nor a tendency amounts to a clear and present danger, since the danger is neither clear not present'.[46] O'Dell goes on to point out that there was nothing in Section 31 to require any degree of imminence – let alone a sufficient degree of imminence – to meet the US Supreme Court test and he concludes: 'As with the old US cases, then, Section 31 can be seen to have been simply an unconstitutional suppression of unpopular political ideas.'

Since Section 31, and in particular the Section 31 orders, were directed towards political material or speech *of any kind* by representatives of the listed organizations (interpreted as encompassing any and all *members* of such organizations) it may legitimately be argued that far from being solely a 'security' measure, the broadcasting ban under Section 31 had a distinctly political purpose. That purpose, at least in part, appears to have been the exclusion from the airwaves of unwelcome political views, and of persons seen as undesirable by those responsible for the ban.

46 O'Dell (see note 25 above).

3 / Disavowing democracy: the silencing project in the South

MARK O'BRIEN

The invoking of Section 31 was only one of a range of legislative measures enacted to cope with the outbreak of the Northern conflict. When looked at holistically, all the legislative measures combined to create a silencing project in the Southern state. The term 'silencing project' carries with it the trappings of a conspiracy theory but essentially refers to the canalling of legislation and government policy so as to amplify one interpretation of a situation and demonize any competing interpretations. The articulation of public opinion is effectively a vocalizing project by citizens or media professionals to articulate a commonly held view that may produce political consequences. A silencing project reflects the reverse of this whereby legislation or government policy makes citizens or media professionals wary of expressing a contrary opinion for fear of attracting a negative sanction or public odium. The concept is derived from Elizabeth Noelle-Newman's Spiral of Silence theory which postulates that society threatens individuals that deviate from the perceived consensus with isolation and exclusion; that individuals have a largely subconscious fear of isolation; that this fear of isolation causes people to constantly check which opinions are approved or disapproved of in their environment; and that the results of these assessments affect people's willingness to speak out. If people believe that their opinion is part of the consensus, they have the confidence to speak out. Conversely, if people feel they are in the minority, they become more cautious and silent. This process may then become a spiral wherein one opinion is routinely expressed in an over-confident manner while other opinions decline in public view save for the exception of a hard core of believers.[1] The notion of a 'silencing project' includes all the above but is the result of a process whereby governments amplify one definition of a situation and repress alternative interpretations either via legislation or by demonizing those that continue to present alternative viewpoints.

The opinion of the Southern population towards the Northern conflict is difficult to qualify as opinion changed as the conflict unfolded. In the 1950s, the IRA's border campaign met with indifference in the South. However, the suppression of the civil rights movement and the pogroms of 1969 galvanized sym-

---

1 Noelle-Neumann, E. (1993) *The spiral of silence: public opinion – our social skin*. Chicago: University of Chicago Press, 201.

pathy and support for the nationalist community. This reached its peak in the aftermath of Bloody Sunday in 1972 when over 50,000 people marched to the British embassy in Dublin and burned it down. From then on the conflict entered its bloodiest phase and although support for the IRA dwindled, there remained the fear within Southern politics that given certain conditions, public opinion could swing back again. The opinions of the Southern electorate towards the North were succinctly captured in a 1978 survey carried out by the Economic and Social Research Institute. As regards the IRA, 60 per cent of respondents opposed IRA activities, 21 per cent supported such activities and 19 per cent remained neutral. In contrast, 42 per cent of respondents supported the motives of the IRA, 33 per cent opposed such motives and 25 per cent remained neutral. On the issue of partition, 72 per cent were anti-partition while 13 per cent were pro-partition. Asked whether the Irish government should put pressure on Britain to withdraw from the North, 64 per cent of respondents agreed while 33 per cent disagreed. Asked if the British government should announce a future withdrawal at a fixed date, 78 per cent agreed and 18 per cent disagreed.[2] From the above statistics it is safe to surmise two things; one, a clear majority rejected the activities of the IRA, and two, a clear majority supported self-determination for the entire island.

Despite the huge gap between these sentiments and the desultory level of support that Sinn Féin attracted at election time, to some these two clear-cut positions could not be separated because a large section of the population remained neutral on the motives of the IRA. The belief was that so long as people stayed neutral, there remained an ambiguity towards violence that could turn into support given certain circumstances. This was the so-called 'leaky national consensus' – the shaky climate of public opinion that republican spokespeople could supposedly manipulate to win support. The argument was simple: spokespeople would exploit broadcasters' obsession with facts – who, what, when, where, how, why – to win over the neutrals and thus never 'lose' an interview. As long as this 'leaky national consensus' or ambiguity existed, Section 31 was needed to prevent such spokespeople from manipulating public opinion.[3] The problem with such a synopsis is that it is based on the model of direct effects and assumes that audience members are passive dupes rather than critically thinking individuals. It assumes that should a spokesperson 'get the better' of an interviewer, then audience members would side with the spokesperson. It also assumes that the interview is the only factor in the formation of opinion. However, audiences interpret media messages through previously formed opinions and prior experiences, and there is a huge difference between 'winning' an interview and winning public support. Nonetheless, this 'leaky national consensus' argument formed the basis of

2 Davis, E. & Sinnott, R. (1979) *Attitudes in the Republic of Ireland relevant to the Northern Ireland problem.* Dublin: Economic and Social Research Institute.   3 Harris, E. (1987) 'Television and terrorism'. Unpublished.

the 'provo-scare' – the belief that people exposed to the voices and viewpoints of republican spokespeople would be won over – and thus provided a justification for Section 31. As a consequence, the complicated disintegration of the Northern state and the subsequent conflict became so simplified in the realm of public discourse that even the mildest support for self-determination was viewed as tacit support for the IRA. Those who sought to widen the debate to include the actions of either state or their security institutions were at best regarded as gullible or at worst viewed as IRA apologists. The legislation and policy of successive governments contributed significantly to this process – the cumulative effect of which was a silencing project. The central element of this silencing project was its normative aspect. The South's governmental response to the conflict did not emerge from a broad and open public debate about the origins or underlying causes of the conflict or what response the South should adopt. Instead, it emerged as a kind of 'received wisdom' or 'common sense' that obviated the need for debate and strongly questioned the motives of anyone who advocated or engaged in such a discussion. This 'common sense' held that the government had the right to take whatever measures it deemed necessary to ensure the survival of the Southern state and that anyone who questioned this doctrine was not fully committed to the maintenance of democracy.

The silencing project was fuelled by the emergence of a siege mentality within the Southern body politic that became manifest in four areas. Firstly, within mainstream politics there was a genuinely held but over-estimated belief that the conflict would engulf the Southern state. As a result the conflict was principally defined not as a political problem but as a law and order issue that the legal system would resolve. Such a definition resulted in the introduction of some of the most repressive legislation in western Europe that impacted on those who viewed the conflict in political terms. Secondly, under pressure to discourage dissent, the Garda Síochána was effectively given a free hand. Frequent allegations of Garda misconduct were met with a policy of see no evil, hear no evil and speak no evil on the part of government. Thirdly, the only institution that could challenge this hegemony – the media – was forcibly silenced on the grounds that interviews with republican spokespeople would incite people to support the IRA. While Section 31 successfully gagged the broadcast media, Section 3 of the Criminal Law Bill attempted but failed to silence the print media. Nonetheless newspapers and periodicals were frequently brought before the courts on spurious charges of contempt. Lastly, any party or individual that expressed concern about any of the above or who peacefully questioned the legitimacy of the Northern state or Britain's role in the conflict was regarded as having ulterior motives. This demonization of alternative viewpoints was a major element in the silencing project by virtue of its chilling effect on public debate.

A STATE UNDER SIEGE

The perception of a state under siege and the consequential belief that the government had the right to take whatever measures it deemed necessary to ensure the survival of the state had its origins in the Arms Crisis of 1969–70. During this period the Fianna Fáil Government authorized the mobilization of the army and its deployment along the border, authorized the movement of a consignment of arms to Dundalk to be distributed to Northern civilians in the event of a 'doomsday scenario', and authorized the training of Derry nationalists in the use of weaponry. It also authorized £100,000 for the 'relief of stress' in the North – a substantial portion of which was paid to a German arms dealer for guns and munitions that were to be flown to Dublin Airport. The issue of whether or not the latter action was government policy has always been hotly debated. Suffice to say that when the plan became public the government line was that it was a plot hatched by a cabal of renegade ministers that was in cahoots with the IRA. Four ministers subsequently left the cabinet, rumours of a coup d'état swept the country and the public's attention was gripped by the events at the Arms Trial. What followed was an avalanche of legislation designed ostensibly to protect the existence of the state but which also had a chilling effect on debate in the South.

In December 1970 the government announced it was considering the introduction of internment, Section 31 was invoked in October 1971 and in May 1972 the Minister for Justice Des O'Malley re-introduced the jury-less Special Criminal Court.[4] The justification for its re-introduction was that the state could no longer rely on jury courts to try those accused of subversive crime because juries were being intimidated. When challenged in the Dáil to cite examples of such intimidation, O'Malley failed to do so. A more likely scenario was that the government feared that in times of high emotion, juries would understand though not necessarily condone the actions of accused individuals and return not guilty verdicts. Much to the government's embarrassment, the jury in the Arms Trial had unanimously returned not guilty verdicts that acquitted the accused and put the spotlight firmly back on the cabinet.[5] Whatever the motive, the public was sidelined and silenced in the administration of justice in such cases. In November 1972, the Offences against the State Amendment Act allowed for a person to be convicted of IRA membership solely on the opinion of a Garda chief superintendent. This shifted the burden of proof from the state to the accused who now had to prove that the Garda's opinion was wrong. In a prophetic attack on the legislation, Labour's Conor Cruise O'Brien criticized the 'drastic powers

4 It was originally established under the Offences against the State Act 1939 and was suspended in 1946.   5 Among some Southern politicians there existed a view that the Arms Trial jury was intimidated. See O'Brien, J. (2000) *The Arms Trial*. Dublin: Gill and Macmillan, 220.

reversing the onus of proof' and surmised that Irish democracy was being 'eroded and curtailed, trampled, constricted and distorted' to the extent that the powers not 'abused this year or next year may well in future circumstances be abused'.[6]

Despite such opposition, the perception of a state under siege gained momentum during the Fine Gael-Labour coalition of 1973-7. When, in July 1976, the IRA assassinated the newly appointed British ambassador Christopher Ewart-Biggs, the government responded with more legislation. The Emergency Powers Bill proclaimed a state of emergency and also allowed for the detention of individuals without charge for seven days if Gardaí had a 'reasonable suspicion' against the individual.[7] The thinking of the government was clearly illustrated by the Minister for Justice, Patrick Cooney, who dismissed fears for civil liberties by declaring that such fears were 'not real fears for people unless they are on the side of the enemies of the state'.[8] One individual with concerns about the bill was President Cearbhall Ó Dálaigh. A former Chief Justice, Ó Dálaigh exercised his prerogative to send the bill to the Supreme Court to test its constitutionality. At a speech at an army barracks, the Minister for Defence, Paddy Donegan, told the assembled units that the President (and commander-in-chief of the armed forces) was 'a thundering disgrace' and that the army 'must stand behind the state'. The outburst implied that such an independently minded President could not be trusted and should a difference develop between the government and the President then the army should back the government. The fact that a Minister had attacked the head of state in front of the armed forces was lost on a government obsessed with security. Taoiseach Liam Cosgrave refused to accept Donegan's resignation and so, stating that the presidency had been compromised by the government's actions, O'Dálaigh resigned. In a state where dealing with the effects rather than the causes of the conflict took precedence, not even the head of state was allowed to express concerns about civil liberties.

TURNING A BLIND EYE

The siege mentality also affected the Garda Síochána as it came under pressure to discourage dissent; a result of which was the increased use of Section 30 of the Offences against the State Act, whereby a person could be arrested and detained solely on the suspicion that he or she was about to or had committed a crime. During the 1970s the increased use of this section to clamp down on dissent is apparent. In 1973, 271 people were arrested and 181 were subsequently charged. In

---

6 O'Toole, F. 'The life and times of Conor Cruise O'Brien' (part three) in *Magill*, June 1986, 37-46.   7 The state of emergency that had existed since 1939 was ended and a new state of emergency was declared. This lasted until February 1995.   8 Dunne, D. & Kerrigan, G. (1984) *Round up the usual suspects*. Dublin: Magill, 184.

1975, 607 people were arrested and 116 charged. The respective figures for 1977 are 1144 and 150, and for 1979 are 1431 and 169. The disparity between those arrested and those charged with an offence illustrates the abuse of the Section towards those who attended meetings and protests that the state viewed as undesirable. More seriously perhaps, from 1975 onwards, allegations of systematic ill-treatment of individuals in Garda custody emerged.

The allegations centred on a specific number of Gardaí and included allegations of sleep deprivation, repeated physical assault and relentless interrogation. By the late 1970s approximately 80 per cent of serious crimes were being 'solved' by confessions alone – many of which were later retracted in court.[9] In his autobiography, the then Minister for Posts and Telegraphs, Conor Cruise O'Brien outlined how Garda misconduct helped solve a kidnapping case. In October 1975, Republicans kidnapped Dutch industrialist Tiede Herrema and demanded the release of republican prisoners. The Gardaí traced the gang to a house and after an eighteen-day standoff Herrema was released unharmed. Shortly after, O'Brien asked his Special Branch bodyguards how the Gardaí had discovered the hideout. One of the detectives replied that a member of the gang had been arrested and while being transferred to Dublin the car transporting him stopped. 'The escort started asking him questions and when at first he refused to answer, they beat the shit out of him. Then he told them where Herrema was.' For fear of worrying his Cabinet colleagues, O'Brien kept the information to himself.[10]

In January 1977, a detainee jumped from a second-floor window of Cahir Garda station – a move allegedly prompted by his desire to escape ill-treatment. Although the incident was mentioned on RTÉ news bulletins, management rejected suggestions by reporters that a film report be compiled or that the man be interviewed, even though he was never charged with any crime.[11] The growing unease led to rumours that a 'Heavy Gang' of interrogators that specialized in the extraction of confessions was operating within the force. The cabinet discussed the allegations and concluded that it would 'be sending very conflicting signals to public opinion if at the same time as enacting [emergency] legislation … we instituted an inquiry into the interrogation of suspects held by the Gardaí'.[12] This despite the fact that one Minister knew that Garda misconduct had helped solve the Herrema kidnapping. Instead of holding an inquiry, the government stated that the allegations were either IRA propaganda or rumours by rogue Gardaí to discredit the government.[13] In February 1977, two senior Gardaí met with the

9 O'Briain Report (1978) *Report of the Committee to Recommend Certain Safeguards for Persons in Custody and for Members of An Garda Síochána*. Dublin: Stationary Office.   10 O'Brien, C.C. (1998) *Memoir: my life and themes*. Dublin: Poolbeg Press, 355.   11 McGurk, T. 'The silent years' in *Sunday Tribune*, 11 January 1981.   12 FitzGerald, G. (1991) *All in a life: an autobiography*. Dublin: Gill & Macmillan, 313.   13 In 2004, Justin Keating, a member of that cabinet, stated in response to allegations of contemporary misconduct, 'I'm satisfied that the nods and winks that were given to the Gardaí at that

Minister for Foreign Affairs, Garret FitzGerald, and told him that they believed that 'confessions had been extracted by improper methods'. According to FitzGerald, he wrote to Taoiseach Liam Cosgrave outlining his concerns but nothing came of it. Shortly after, the *Irish Times* published a series of articles that identified the sections of the Garda Síochána to which members of the Heavy Gang were attached. It also extensively catalogued the injuries sustained by suspects.[14]

The exposé held the front page for three days and – despite the knowledge within the cabinet that things were not quite right, it again denied the veracity of the story. The Minster for Justice, Patrick Cooney, condemned the 'gullible and uninformed media' that had been 'taken in by people whose interests are served by breaking down pubic confidence in the police'.[15] For its part, RTÉ felt obliged to help restore such confidence. In April 1977, an RTÉ crew was sent to cover a protest outside Portlaoise prison. Having been instructed not to record sound, the footage turned out to be useless when the protest turned into a serious riot and the station was forced to borrow film from the BBC for its nightly news bulletin. As journalists put the package together, senior executives rang the news desk instructing that the film be edited so as not to give the impression of 'Garda brutality'. Amnesty International's investigation into the allegations concluded that 'maltreatment appears to have been carried out systematically by detectives who appear to specialise in the use of oppressive methods in extracting statements from persons suspected of involvement in serious politically motivated crimes'. The report also criticized the Special Criminal Court for failing or refusing to scrutinise allegations of ill-treatment closely enough.[16]

PRESS CENSORSHIP

A crucial by-product of this siege mentality was the implementation of state-sponsored censorship that attempted to ensure that only one interpretation of the conflict was reflected in the media. Initially this censorship was restricted to the broadcast media; the origins, justifications, arguments against and consequences of it are examined in other chapters. In July 1976 the Fine Gael-Labour coalition attempted to impose a similar ban on the print media. Section 3 of the Criminal Law Bill consisted of a highly ambiguous definition of incitement that was aimed at curtailing the reporting of the conflict as a political battle. In particular, the section was aimed at the *Irish Press* because within the coalition 'there was a feeling that the *Irish Press* was subversive to the state; that it was justifying

time gave rise to the culture we see today': Coulter, C. 'Opportunity to reform Garda Síochána must not be missed' in *Irish Times*, 17 January 2004. **14** See *Irish Times*, 14 February 1977. **15** Allen, G. (1999) *The Garda Síochána: policing independent Ireland, 1922-82*. Dublin: Gill & Macmillan, 193. **16** Report of Amnesty International Mission to Ireland 1977.

and provoking IRA killings'.[17] But Section 3 was so ambiguously worded that any report, interview, feature, editorial or letter to the editor could be judged to fall within its remit on a trial-by-trial basis.

> Any person who, expressly or by implication, directly or through another person or persons, or by advertisement, propaganda or any other means, incites or invites another person (or other persons generally) to join an unlawful organisation or to take part in, support or assist its activities shall be guilty of an offence and shall be liable on conviction on indictment to imprisonment for a term not exceeding ten years.[18]

In an interview with Bernard Nossitor of the *Washington Post*, Conor Cruise O'Brien stated that the South had a 'cultural problem' in relation to the IRA and the North. This consisted of 'a whole framework of teaching, of ballads of popular awe that enabled the IRA to survive, even to flourish and most of all to recruit young and impressionable people'.[19] In the course of the interview O'Brien produced a bunch of readers' letters to the *Irish Press* that he believed represented this 'wrong-headed culture' and indicated his determination to tackle the medium that printed them. The Attorney General, Declan Costello, later confirmed to the paper's political correspondent that 'if the *Irish Press* continued to print such letters then he would charge the editor'.[20] This intention to suppress the opinions of ordinary people who had written letters to a newspaper was indicative of how far the government was prepared to go to silence alternative viewpoints. In a subsequent Dáil debate, O'Brien stated that newspapers were the IRA's favourite medium of 'recruitment propaganda' and that once Section 3 of the new bill became law it would pose no threat to newspapers, as they would be too afraid to publish anything that might be interpreted as breaching the section. This, according to O'Brien, would result in a 'significant diminution in the publication of pro-IRA propaganda'.[21]

The section would also have curtailed the ability of newspapers to interview members of Sinn Féin, to report court cases or to editorialize on the conflict, and a campaign by the NUJ to have the words that could be interpreted as pertaining to the print media deleted (from 'who' to 'incites') was eventually successful. But despite the coalition's unsuccessful attempt to gag the print media, the chilling effect remained and several publications were summoned before the courts. In 1975 the Special Criminal Court declared itself 'scandalised' after the *Irish Press* published claims that Gardaí had beaten up suspects. Its editor, Tim Pat

---

17 *Irish Press* political correspondent Michael Mills cited in O'Brien, M. (2001) *De Valera, Fianna Fáil and the* Irish Press. Dublin: Irish Academic Press, 149. 18 *Dáil Éireann Debates* 292 (1976) col. 482. 19 O'Brien, M., op. cit., 149. 20 Ibid. 21 *Dáil Éireann Debates* 292 (1976) cols 474-9.

Coogan, was prosecuted but successfully defended the newspaper. In 1976 the editor of the *Irish Times*, Fergus Pyle, was charged with contempt after the paper reproduced terminology from a press release that referred to the Special Criminal Court as a 'sentencing tribunal'. In similar vein, the fortnightly magazine, *Hibernia*, was summoned to appear before the court after publishing a reader's letter that had referred to a trial there, putting the word 'trial' in quotation marks. The publication was faced with contempt of court proceedings and the assistant editor with responsibility for editing readers' letters, Brian Trench, was required to purge that contempt with a formal apology to the court. Such reactions demonstrate how overly sensitive the institutions of the state were to scrutiny and criticism during the 1970s.

DEMONISATION OF ALTERNATIVE VIEWPOINTS

All of the foregoing combined to foster the strongly held conviction within the body politic that there was only one way of reading the conflict in the North. That reading was wholly encapsulated in virulent condemnation of the IRA. This emphasis on the actions of one party to the conflict had a de-contextualizing effect as it concentrated on the effects rather than the causes of the conflict. Also, as latter-day revelations have demonstrated, it allowed another party to the conflict to evade media scrutiny and engage in what is euphuistically termed a 'dirty war'. Adding fuel to this belief was the crossover of revisionism – a form of historical investigation characterized by value-free analysis that sought to critically interrogate the nationalist narrative of Ireland's struggle for independence – from the discipline of history to the realm of journalism. While traditional historiography viewed the conflict as the culmination of an historical process, revisionism viewed it as a result of extremism fuelled by nationalist myths about the struggle for liberation. Taken to extremes, revisionism was anti-nationalist and viewed any celebration of nationhood or commemoration of independence in the South as glorifying and encouraging violence perpetrated for political ends. Hence the belief that the celebrations held in Dublin in 1966 to commemorate the fiftieth anniversary of the 1916 Rising and the broadcasting of *Insurrection* by RTÉ that same year acted as catalysts for the conflict that erupted in 1969 (this despite the fact that the vast majority of Northern homes could not receive RTÉ's transmission signal). A more realistic analysis would point to the historical discrimination against nationalists, the suppression of the civil rights movement and the events of Bloody Sunday as crystallizing points of the conflict.

Nonetheless anti-nationalist revisionism became a dominant force in much of the Southern media; its advocates were as energetic in expressing their own views as they were in dismissing any contrasting views. In particular the Workers' Party promoted a pro-Section 31 anti-nationalist analysis of the conflict and members or supporters of the party exerted disproportionate influence in RTÉ and the *Irish Times*. In a wider media context, commentators or journalists who advocated a more critical analysis of the conflict or who campaigned for the repeal of Section 31 were viewed with suspicion or accused of harbouring IRA sympathies. The volume of abusive labels devised to discredit such individuals is mind-boggling. Terms such as fellow-traveller, sneaking-regarder, provo-stooge, crypto-provo and hush-puppy-provo entered the lexicon used to label critically thinking individuals as IRA apologists. One of the more public manifestations of this phenomena occurred in 1974 when a Minister made an after-dinner speech to political correspondents and accused them of being 'provo-stooges' because of their coverage of the conflict.[22]

A REPUBLIC OF SILENCE

When considered in isolation, the emergence of a siege mentality, the repressive legislation, the turning of a blind eye to abuses perpetrated by agents of the state, the heavy-handed censorship of broadcasting, the attempted censorship of print media and the virulent demonization of any views that challenged the conventional wisdom on the conflict may appear as phenomena unrelated to one another. However, when considered together, the cumulative effect was to create and perpetuate a climate of silence and fear of expressing opinions or analyses that went against the pseudo-consensus that the only permissible and safe thing to say on the conflict was to condemn the IRA.

The net result was zero public pressure on the Southern body politic to actively engage with what was happening north of the border. Conversely, the IRA never had to account for its actions or place its activities in a political rather than a military context. In short, the demands of censorship prevented the nation from adequately addressing the conflict from which the ban arose. The most proffered justification for Section 31 was that those who refuted the democratic process also forfeited the rights – including the right to freedom of expression – of that democracy. However, it is equally arguable that those who stifled debate also refuted or had no faith in the democratic process. This curtailment of debate not only impacted on people's ability to talk about the conflict, it also severely hampered the ability of the broadcasting media to test and establish the truth of many occurrences of the conflict. This in turn further diluted the robust public

22 Anon. 'Conor Cruise O'Brien and the Media' in *Belfast Bulletin* (9) Spring 1981, 2–8.

debate that is necessary for any properly functioning democracy. The over-whelming determination on the part of successive governments to limit rather than encourage critical debate resulted in the conflict being publicly defined in black and white terms for over two decades. One of the most damning and iron-ic consequences of such one-dimensional thinking was that successive govern-ments unwittingly fell into their own trap of silence. For fear of exciting an eas-ily influenced Southern electorate and inciting support for the IRA, successive governments could only offer the most insipid responses to injustices such as the imprisonment of the Birmingham Six and the Guildford Four and the Dublin and Monaghan bombings. Indeed, the fact that the annual renewal of Section 31 usually passed without any debate in Dáil Éireann is itself a testament to the asphyxiating silence that characterized the Southern response to the Northern conflict.

Part II

Censorship and journalistic practice

4 / Getting tough with RTÉ

DESMOND FISHER

In the not too distant future, when the obituaries of public service broadcasting, as we now know it are being written, Section 31 will possibly merit only a passing reference. At the time, of course, the legislation had important repercussions among the broadcasters themselves and on their dealings with the governments of the 1970s, 1980s and into the 1990s.

The Section 31 legislation was designed primarily to deprive Northern Ireland paramilitaries and their political wings of the publicity that radio and television broadcasting would give them. Whatever success it achieved in this, the effect of the legislation was to deny the public access to the information and comment to which the broadcasters believed they were entitled, even though most of the audience may have agreed with the restriction placed on RTÉ. The threat of the legislation also encouraged ministers to interfere more often in the broadcasting organization and fostered a 'get tough with RTÉ' attitude, later demonstrated by Ray Burke's attempts to strangle the organization, precipitating a financial crisis that may yet contribute to its collapse.

As things turned out, Section 31 probably gave the Provisional IRA and Sinn Féin more publicity than they would have got if the ban had not been imposed and in the light of subsequent developments may even have strengthened Sinn Féin support in the general public. It was ironic that some of the people banned from the Irish airwaves were later to be feted at the White House and even to be officially received by successors of the government that had banned them.

Above all, the enactment of the Section 31 legislation highlighted the dilemma that has bedevilled the relationship between government and broadcasters from the beginning of radio broadcasting in Ireland in 1926 and more urgently after the setting up of the television service on the last day of 1960: is public service broadcasting an arm of the government of the day, committed to supporting whatever action that government takes, or do the broadcasters share with the independent press the role of public watchdog, exercising the right of the people to information and the right of the media to impart it and to comment on the issues of the day?

The 1960 Act, which set up RTÉ and which remains the main piece of broadcasting legislation, did not address this question. The Act gave the organization a relatively large measure of autonomy, only two clauses making specific provisions as regards programming. Section 18 required the RTÉ Authority 'to ensure that broadcasting relating to matters of public controversy or the subject of current public debate should be presented objectively and impartially and without any expression of the Authority's own views'.

Section 31 (1) of the Act empowered the Minister for Posts and Telegraphs 'to direct the Authority in writing (1) to refrain from broadcasting any particular matter or matter of any particular class, and (2) to allocate broadcasting time for announcements by or on behalf of any Minister of State in connection with the functions of that Minister'. Formally speaking, therefore, a Section 31 direction was a statutory or ministerial order issued in exercise of the powers conferred by Section 31 (1) of the Broadcasting Authority Act 1960 (No. 10 of 1960).[1]

Given the place of politics in Ireland, it was inevitable that in its early days RTÉ, like other semi-state bodies, would experience occasional political interference, though for the most part in a minor key. Politicians complained about the coverage or lack of coverage of their local areas; Irish language groups demanded more Irish programming; rural people charged RTÉ with having a Dublin bias. But after a few more serious confrontations with individual politicians, Seán Lemass articulated the government attitude to RTÉ. He is frequently quoted as saying that RTÉ was 'an arm of government'. In fact, his statement was more nuanced but still uncomfortable for the broadcasters. He told the Dáil in 1966 that:

> Radio Telefís Éireann was set up by legislation as an instrument of public policy and as such is responsible to the Government ... The Government reject the view that RTÉ ... should be, either generally or in regard to its current affairs and news programmes, completely independent of Government supervision. It has the duty, while maintaining impartiality between political parties ... to sustain public respect for the institutions of government and, where appropriate, to assist public understanding of the policies enshrined in legislation enacted by the Oireachtas. The Government will take such action ... as may be necessary to ensure that RTÉ does not deviate from the due performance of this duty.[2]

This enigmatic pronouncement, that governments ever since have been tempted to interpret as a licence to treat RTÉ as their policy tool, ensured a continuing uneasy relationship between them. RTÉ did not reply directly to Lemass' assertion at the time. But later, in a booklet called *A View of Irish Broadcasting*, written in 1971 though not published until 1973, it articulated its own understanding of broadcasting's function in society. In a classic exposition of the function of public service broadcasting, it said:

---

1 After this Act was amended, the words 'inserted by Section 16 of the Broadcasting Authority (Amendment) Act, 1976 (No. 37 of 1976)' were added.   2 *Dáil Éireann Debates* 224 (1966) col. 1046.

> The preservation of the status quo is not necessarily always in the public interest: neither is the public interest necessarily always in complete harmony with every action or lack of action by government. A democratic society assumes that its broadcasting system should serve the public interest.

More serious crises arose in relation to an RTÉ proposal to send a television team to North Vietnam in 1967 and the recall of another team *en route* to Biafra some time later. A major confrontation took place in 1969 over the broadcast of a TV programme dealing with illegal money lending in Dublin. In a characteristic example of shooting the messenger, the government set up a judicial tribunal that sat for fifty days, examined 141 witnesses and cost an estimated £250,000 without resulting in any alleviation of the problem the programme exposed. The affair was a traumatic experience for RTÉ and exemplified the difference between the sort of evidence that broadcasting relies on for its programmes and the sort of evidence the judicial process demands.[3]

The most serious confrontations between RTÉ and the government came in the context of the Northern Ireland 'Troubles' of the past three decades when the Minister for Posts and Telegraphs (as the post was then known) took serious and public action against the broadcasting organization. The outbreak of the 'Northern Troubles' in 1969 had good and bad consequences for RTÉ news coverage. At first, it put extra strains on the News Division that was under-equipped with staff and technical resources in the North to deal with events there.

In the early stages, the real dimensions of the developments were not fully appreciated and reporters and camera crews were sent north for a day or so at a time. As the situation worsened, the then Head of News, Jim McGuinness, argued forcibly that what was happening was of historical importance and future generations would be examining the archives to see how RTÉ had risen to the challenge. Eventually, the News Division got the extra manpower, offices and facilities it needed and news and current affairs coverage of the North were greatly improved. To strengthen editorial controls, RTÉ appointed four duty editors to the newsroom. These were senior journalists, one of who would be on duty during broadcasting hours to adjudicate on difficult editorial decisions.

Ironically, it was not long before complaints began to come in from listeners and viewers about what was categorized as excessive attention to the North. Now that Northern Ireland developments are a regular part of media coverage, it is difficult to appreciate the reaction of so many people in the Republic. It was not so much that they were positively antagonistic to regarding Northern Ireland as part of the country; rather was it that they did not consider events there as of interest and concern.

3 The tribunal concluded that the programme had not provided legally convincing evidence for its allegations.

More news and current affairs broadcasting meant more potential pitfalls for RTÉ and provided scope for more confrontations between the government and the broadcasters. In covering the developments in Northern Ireland, the broadcasters considered it essential to interview spokespersons for Official and Provisional IRA, the different Protestant paramilitary forces and their political wings. This exposure caused concern to the government, which considered that RTÉ interviewers could not adequately cope with well-trained apologists for paramilitary actions and propaganda. On 1 October 1971, after several such interviews, the Minister for Posts and Telegraphs, Gerard Collins, exercised his rights under Section 31 (1) of the Broadcasting Authority Act and in a statutory order directed RTÉ in writing:

> to refrain from broadcasting any matter that could be calculated to promote the aims and activities of any organization which engages in, promotes, encourages or advocates the attainment of any particular objective by violent means.

Next day, the RTÉ Authority issued a public statement drawing attention to 'the inherent difficulties of executing a direction couched in such general terms' and expressing its determination 'to continue to endeavour to provide a balanced, comprehensive broadcasting service which would be authentic in itself and fully responsive to the needs of the whole community within the added constraints of the direction'. Two weeks later, the chairman wrote to the Minister explaining the Authority's own 'specific interpretations' of the Order, which it considered 'appropriate' to help its staff comply with it.

Describing the order as 'so imprecise as to be unsatisfactory in principle and to place an unfair burden' on the Authority, it 'assumed', with some irony, that the 'Government would not intend that RTÉ should not broadcast, for example, interviews with or statements from members of the various Liberation Movements around the world such as the Bangla Desh movement in East Pakistan and Arab national movements in the middle east'. It pointed out that Irish newspapers 'regularly carry material equivalent to what RTÉ could not now apparently carry in the form of broadcast matter'. It interpreted the order as 'essentially concerned with Irish affairs' and insisted that 'a comprehensive, authentic and balanced service of news and public affairs programmes must, within the added constraints of the direction, continue to be provided'.

In explaining the way the organization would interpret the order in programming, it considered that 'the direction does not affect the broadcasting of news material which is reportage and analysis of violent events even where the event is stated to be the action of an organization of the type referred to in the direction'.

Further, 'the direction does not affect the broadcasting of statements from organizations accepting or denying responsibility for violent or other unlawful activities'. And in relation to current affairs programming, where the greatest dangers lay of breaching the order, it said: 'The direction does not prohibit current affairs programmes which feature the activities and policies of the organizations in question included as being relevant to the scope of such programmes, provided the strictest care is taken to have the matter handled in such a manner that reasonable people would not regard the programmes as promoting the aims or activities of these organizations.' The letter ended with a paragraph that would prove prophetic: 'The Authority,' it said, 'considers that practical experience in the period immediately ahead will provide a basis for further clarification of the direction.'

In his reply, the Minister dismissed the Authority's concerns and said he did not consider it proper 'to enter into correspondence on the subject of the direction, which speaks for itself' and therefore he would not comment on the content of the Authority's letter. Repeated attempts to get confirmation of whether or not the Authority's interpretation of the order was acceptable to the Minister proved fruitless and broadcasters found it difficult to construe it in programming terms.

Three times in 1972, RTÉ coverage of Northern affairs was the subject of questions in the Dáil. Towards the end of that year, on Sunday, 19 November, an item on the lunchtime radio news feature programme contained a summary of an interview with Seán Mac Stiofáin, then chief of staff of the Provisional IRA. RTÉ did not broadcast his voice but the reporter involved, Kevin O'Kelly, news feature editor, gave Mac Stiofáin's answers in indirect speech. This attempt to avoid an infringement of the ministerial order did not succeed. Instead, it brought down the government's wrath. Two days after the broadcast, the Minister, still Gerard Collins, wrote to the RTÉ Authority demanding that it meet forthwith to consider what action it intended to take on foot of what he regarded as a direct contravention of his order.

The Authority's reply referred back to its interpretation of the original ministerial order and recalled the Minister's refusal to comment on it. It said that since then RTÉ had provided 'authentic information' about developments in the North, 'requiring hundreds of hours of reportage and analysis, dealing not only with the political, social, religious and physical aspects of events, but also with the prominent organizations and personalities concerned, including those involved in violence'. The letter went on to say the Authority considered that its staff 'has shown a remarkable devotion to duty and a high sense of responsibility in carrying out this immensely difficult and dangerous task' and believed that the radio and television services 'have thus contributed significantly to a fuller understanding of the national situation'.

Pointing out that the method used in the programme concerned – interviewing persons beforehand and reporting their replies – had been used on a previous programme without criticism, it said that it considered the method was in accordance with the specific interpretations it had provided to the Minister on foot of his original order. These interpretations, it added, 'gave practical expression to its [the Authority's] concern fully to implement the direction while maintaining a comprehensive and authentic information service'. Nevertheless, the Authority concluded – without giving any detailed explanation for so doing – 'that the editorial decisions taken showed defective judgement in the context of the direction, a conclusion which is being conveyed to all concerned'. It added that it was satisfied that there was 'no question of *mala fides* on the part of any of its staff who had responsibility for the programme and indeed there were extraneous factors quite beyond the control of the staff which undoubtedly had an adverse effect on the actual presentation'. It ended its letter by undertaking that 'no critical material of the type in question on Sunday last will be broadcast without prior clearance in detail' at Director General level.

While it is probable that no action that the Authority might have taken, short of dismissing most of the current affairs staff, would have satisfied the politicians, it might have been better for the future of the organization if it had adopted a stronger line. If the reply it made was intended to mollify the government, it failed. Describing its letter as 'long-winded and waffling', the Minister, in exercise of the government's powers under Article 6 of the 1960 Act, promptly sacked the Authority and immediately appointed a new body more sympathetic to the government's views. O'Kelly was brought before the Special Criminal Court where he followed standard journalistic practice and refused to name the source for his report. He was sentenced to three months in prison for contempt of court but was let out after one or two nights.[4]

To avoid further difficulties with the government, the new RTÉ Authority decided to draw up guidelines to assist staff in complying with the direction. These were drafted by John Irvine, Deputy Director General, and myself as Deputy Head of News at the time, and were issued for staff in the news and current affairs areas on 15 December 1972. They accepted that 'the requirements of the direction must take precedence and will at times entail departures from normal broadcasting practice'. Matter prohibited from being broadcast under the government's direction would be interpreted by RTÉ as 'matter which in its view would promote the aims and activities of the Provisional IRA, the Official IRA and any other organization or group which may from time to time be adjudged by RTÉ to be covered by the terms of the direction'.

---

4 His sentence was later commuted to a £250 fine.

Procedures were also required in broadcasting matter connected with the two Sinn Féin organizations and other Northern Ireland groups. However, they insisted that factual reportage about all the organizations was not affected by the direction and that statements from them on significant developments could be reported and mute film or stills used, though sound recordings or sound-on-film could not be used in the case of the paramilitaries. When any proposed treatment in news or programmes of the organizations named in the direction was contemplated, broadcasters had to refer up the line for clearance. The document specifically stated that the guidelines were not to be regarded as comprehensive and definite, since it would be impossible to foresee all circumstances. They would be kept under constant review.

In practice, compliance with the direction meant that in case of doubt reporters and producer/directors consulted with their editors who, if necessary, sought guidance in turn from their own superiors to approve any broadcast treatment that might come under the terms of the direction. The main persons responsible for ensuring the direction was observed were the editors of news and current affairs programmes, duty editors in the newsroom, programme editors in the Radio and Television Programmes Divisions and the Heads of these Divisions. Inevitably, the introduction of the guidelines was resented by many of the broadcasters as censorship though some of them recognized that they were necessary to meet the criticism not only from the politicians but also from the majority of the broadcasting audiences. In line with them, RTÉ discontinued direct interviews with spokesmen for the different paramilitary organizations and their political wings. However, it continued to provide intensive news and current affairs coverage of the escalating violence in Northern Ireland in the terms of its own interpretation of the ministerial order.

Governments that consider the nation or themselves in danger will inevitably seek to censor the dissemination of information they consider unhelpful. Whether or not the 'Northern Troubles' constituted such a danger to the Republic as to justify the sacking of an RTÉ Authority and the blanket ban on the sort of reporting RTÉ sought to provide for its audiences is disputable. At the time, some political observers believed that the action of the government was influenced by fierce pressure from the British government on the Irish authorities to take much firmer action against the IRA.

The sacking of the Authority – decided on at cabinet level two days before the Taoiseach, Jack Lynch, went to meet the British Prime Minister in London – came as a bombshell on RTÉ. Some of the staff complained of censorship and the NUJ conducted a long but unsuccessful campaign to have the restrictions lifted. Others believed that the direction had the opposite effect to that intended in that it gave the affected organizations, especially Sinn Féin, an advantage.

They could say what they liked and be reported as saying it but the capacity to question them incisively on air was limited. A minority of RTÉ staff supported the government's action. The relationship between government and RTÉ continued to be marked by suspicion and edginess as broadcasters sought to maintain the quality of northern news and current affairs coverage. Inevitably however, programmes were affected as newsmen and producers learned to tread warily in dealing with Northern developments.

A year after the sacking of the Authority, RTÉ embarked on an organizational change designed to improve current affairs coverage only to have it become a casualty of the next major confrontation with the government. By this time, the Lynch government had been defeated and a Fine Gael-Labour coalition was in office with Conor Cruise O'Brien as the new Minister for Posts and Telegraphs. The proposed change was that all current affairs programmes on radio and television, both those originating in the News Division and those produced in the Programmes Division, be brought together in a new Current Affairs Grouping.

This was not a direct result of the O'Kelly affair but was introduced by way of an experiment to solve a conflict of interest between the news and programme areas – and their respective unions – over the coverage of what is called 'current affairs'. The majority of these programmes were produced by the Programmes Division where most of the producers and production assistants belonged to the Workers' Union of Ireland or to Equity. Other current affairs programmes were produced in the News Division where almost all the journalists belonged to the NUJ. The intention behind the move was to end the union rivalry and to provide a way in which current affairs programmes could have the benefit of professional production skills and at the same time make full use of journalists whether in the News Division or attached to the Grouping itself.

It was not the best time to propose controversial new arrangements for bringing all current affairs programming under one controller. Not all of the new Authority members were in favour of the move and some of the staff in both the News and Programme Divisions opposed it. Since the Deputy Head of News, namely myself, was appointed to head the new group, the Programme Division producers felt they would be no better off than under the Head of News. At the same time, some of the News Division journalists felt that their own news feature programmes covering current affairs were being handed over to producers who belonged to another union. However, it was decided to go ahead with the new arrangement. It was called the Current Affairs Grouping and given quasi-Divisional status in the organization, reporting to the Deputy Director General.

However, there was a major weakness in the new arrangement that I had pointed out to the Director General before it came into operation. This was that the Grouping had no separate establishment of producers, directors, reporters, camera crews and the other staff needed to produce radio and television documentaries and other sophisticated current affairs programmes. These had to be seconded from the radio and television programme Divisions whose Controllers would be unlikely to part easily with a substantial part of their own establishments, especially since, in the general climate of the time, current affairs programmes needed only the most competent and committed people.

The new Grouping came into being in October 1973 and had a difficult year before the next serious clash with the government occurred. This was the broadcast on 17 October 1974, of a *Seven Days* programme dealing with internment in the North, a topical feature since the Long Kesh internment camp outside Lisburn had been burned down two days previously. The preliminary publicity for the programme had indicated that it would consist of a filmed sequence on the chronological development of internment and would be complemented by another programme the following evening that would provide an opportunity for comment on it. Both the programme producer and the editor of the *Seven Days* team did not consider that it would conflict with the Section 31 ministerial order and consequently they decided that it did not need to be referred to me for clearance in compliance with the internal RTÉ guidelines concerning treatment of matters covered in the ministerial order. In fact, the two hours of footage from a UK production company that was to be edited for the main part of the programme did not arrive in Dublin until a few hours before transmission and there was insufficient time to edit it with the normal degree of care. The programme included sequences that, while they may not have been in conflict with the letter of the direction, were emotionally charged and certainly not in line with the highly-antagonist attitude to the republican movement of Dr Conor Cruise O'Brien. Not having been warned in advance, I saw the programme for the first time on transmission and felt it certainly would invite reaction.

It came very quickly. As the Current Affairs Grouping was providing extensive radio and TV coverage of the event, I had arranged to go to Galway next day for the annual conference of the Labour Party. That evening at a reception for conference delegates, the Minister attacked me publicly, telling me that that was the last time I would ever broadcast such a programme. The following evening, when a follow-up discussion was screened to discuss the earlier programme, Dr O'Brien attacked me again, though when I asked him, he admitted that he had not seen either programme. Some days later, he castigated the Director General and his Deputy, asking sarcastically, 'Was the Provisional IRA present when that programme was being made?' The consequences for the Current Affairs Grouping were fatal. After an internal inquiry, the programme producer was disciplined, the editor of the Grouping was reprimanded for 'inadequate and unsustainable' arrangements for production and transmission and I, as Head of the Grouping, was criticized for not ensuring that the appropriate guidelines were adequately observed.

From my point of view, the internal inquiry failed to address what I had described as the 'original sin' of the Current Affairs Grouping, namely the failure to give it its own establishment of producers, presenters and other staff. Finally, after another year of continuing problems in a 'make do' situation with no proper staffing, facilities or accommodation, I proposed that unless these were provided the Grouping should be disbanded and the programmes be dispersed back to the News and Programmes Divisions. This was done, the arrangement lasting for another twenty-six years until early 2002 when news and current affairs programmes were once again brought under the control of the Head of News.

In 1976 the Oireachtas passed an amended Broadcasting Authority Act about which the Minister, Dr Cruise O'Brien, wrote in his autobiography that 'in drafting the legislation the principle on which I worked was one of *limited liberalization*' (the italics are his). The Act removed from the Minister the power of sacking the RTÉ Authority, and amended the Section 31 order to specifically prohibit interviews or reports of interviews with a spokesman or spokesmen for the Provisional IRA, Official IRA, Provisional Sinn Féin, or organizations proscribed in Northern Ireland. The naming of the groups included in the ban was an improvement on the previous wording and revised guidelines were issued to cover the new situation. In February 1982, when RTÉ wanted to allot time to Sinn Féin for a party political broadcast in the general election, the Supreme Court ruled against it. Earlier in 1982, Patrick Cooney, the Minister for Posts and Telegraphs in the Fine Gael-Labour coalition, had issued a stronger direction. This directed RTÉ to refrain from broadcasting any matter that was:

a) a broadcast, whether purporting to be a political party broadcast or not, made by or on behalf of or advocating, offering or inviting support for the organization styling itself Sinn Féin;
b) a broadcast by any person or persons representing or purporting to represent the organization styling itself Sinn Féin.

In 1983, the then Minister, Mr Jim Mitchell, issued another direction which in addition banned the Ulster Defence Association, the INLA and 'any organization which in Northern Ireland is a proscribed organization for the purpose of Section 21 of the Act of the British Parliament entitled the Northern Ireland (Emergency Provisions) Act 1978'.

So draconian was RTÉ's interpretation of the directions and so meticulous its observance of the guidelines concerning them that broadcasters were prevented from interviewing on radio or television programmes not merely 'a person or persons representing' Sinn Féin but any member of the organization even if the broadcast concerned matters totally unconnected with politics. Gerry Adams was not permitted on air to talk about a book of short stories he had written. Sinn Féin politicians engaged in industrial unrest were barred from discussing on air aspects of their action and even a Sinn Féin member who kept bees could not be interviewed on his hobby. In 1992, Mr Justice O'Hanlon in the High Court was to find this extension of censorship 'bad in law, a misconstruction of the law and null and void'. Some criticism of RTÉ surfaced in 1982 for covering the deaths of ten hunger strikers less comprehensively than did the BBC and ITV while in 1988 a radio reporter lost her job for including in her report Martin McGuinness' order for the tricolours on the coffins of the three IRA members shot in Gibraltar to be removed when the cortege was crossing the border into Northern Ireland. In 1994, after the Provisional IRA declared a ceasefire, the ministerial order under Section 31 was allowed to lapse.

In retrospect, it would be difficult to approve of the legislation wholeheartedly or to disagree with it completely. Certainly most of RTÉ's listeners and viewers seem to have supported the government's actions though that may have been because they had grown bored with northern coverage rather than because they resented the publicity the paramilitaries got. However, the banning of individuals or organizations on an *a priori* basis is, arguably, not something for a broadcasting organization to determine. If the government decides that publicity of any sort is unacceptable it should proscribe the organizations – and ban both the press and the broadcasters from giving them any kind of publicity – rather than censor only the broadcasters. Governments, however, are chary of interfering directly with the printed media; the privately owned press can prove a powerful enemy.

The relationship between Irish public service broadcasters and government has never been easy and it is not likely to be completely satisfactory to either side. But it is not just in Ireland that difficulties in determining the function of public service broadcasting *vis-à-vis* the government exist. Wherever there is a public service broadcasting organization, the struggle between it and the national politicians continues, as was exemplified in the bitter dispute between the BBC and No. 10 Downing Street in the summer of 2003 over Prime Minister Blair's justification of the 2003 war on Iraq.

Unfortunately, developments in information technology militate against this dilemma being solved, jeopardizing the future of public broadcasting with its remit of serving the public interest. The multiplication of radio and television has led to a decline in serious programming and television especially is rapidly becoming a medium of entertainment only, leading to the neglect of the two other roles of information and education that Lord Reith defined as broadcasting's function. The licence fee is the lifeblood of the public broadcaster. If a public, sated with independent channels less likely to transmit challenges to the status quo, rebels against a charge for listening and viewing, governments will be tempted to cancel the licence fee. That would mark the end of public service broadcasting which many politicians seem to perceive as the real opposition to their policies.

The core of the problem is that governments wish and expect that the editorial judgements of public service broadcasters on matters of public interest should correspond with their own editorial judgments on those matters. Matters of public interest are not, of course, all matters that the general public is interested in; they are matters that relate to the common good. And this is an area in which broadcasters and politicians do not always agree. The RTÉ statement already quoted in reply to the Lemass broadside made this clear, although in an understandably more tactful way, when it said that 'the preservation of the status quo is not necessarily always in the public interest: neither is the public interest necessarily always in complete harmony with every action or lack of action by government'. The public broadcaster based its claim on the grounds that 'a democratic society assumes that its broadcasting system should serve the public interest', not the interests of the government of the day.

It follows that the real question at issue here, as in the Section 31 confrontations in RTÉ, is that there are really no precise rules that can be devised to regulate the relationship of governments to public service broadcasters. In the case of RTÉ, the case can be made that in no instance did RTÉ breach the letter of the regulations in the Broadcasting Acts and the ministerial orders. It could, however, be argued that RTÉ breached the *spirit* of the law. This, of course, is so imprecise as to provide no guidance to the broadcasters as to how they should determine their course of action in any particular instance and the absence of any clear wording leaves the government free to put any construction it likes on the broadcaster's actions.

The Broadcasting Act 2001 formally repealed Section 31 and the indications are that the government might decide to distance itself from the present close relationship with RTÉ by turning it into a commercial state company incorporated under the Companies Act and answerable to a single broadcasting authority alongside the independent radio and TV stations. This would mean that, as far as restriction of any kind is concerned, RTÉ would be treated in the same way as the independent media, subject to no interference except by way of pre-emptive censorship or of post-publication recourse to libel and defamation laws.

5 / Censorship, not 'self-censorship'

COLUM KENNY

The debate about Section 31 has never been purely theoretical. There are murderous people who mouth democratic and libertarian sentiments while plotting to do whatever may be necessary to get their own way. They have hatred in their hearts and blood on their hands, and they are prepared to manipulate the media in order to achieve their objectives. It is the responsibility of journalists to disclose that reality to the public, as much as it is also their responsibility to interrogate the powerful organs of state.

Journalists ought to be activists for the truth, regardless of their own opinions about the political options facing society. However, not everyone who has a view on Section 31 is able to see far beyond the prism of their particular prejudice or political inclination. Journalists who let personal agendas distort or supersede their responsibility to tell the truth are betraying their profession. There is a difference between opposing Section 31 because its existence might hinder the advancement of a particular party or cause, and opposing Section 31 because it inhibits an understanding of the truth.

In my opinion, any journalist worth her or his salt will support the freedom to choose whom to interview or to quote when reporting known facts. I will say more later about 'truth', 'professionalism' and 'facts' as concepts. But, first, I wish to consider how, in practice, Section 31 impinged for years on the freedom of choice of journalists working in Irish broadcasting.

THE CHILLING EFFECT OF SECTION 31

When I joined RTÉ in 1977 there was no choice in respect of recording or transmitting certain kinds of interview. Under Section 31, journalists and producers at the station were forbidden to interview members of Sinn Féin or of certain other organizations, even if it was believed that the inclusion of such interviews in a report was necessary to tell the full story, and even if what the members of those organizations had to say did not constitute an incitement to violence. During the following years, as I worked as a reporter and presenter on various radio and television programmes, there were times when the ban on such interviews seemed particularly ludicrous.

For example, I recall one particular occasion in east Belfast, when I sat in a working-men's club with a group of tough dockers who were Protestants. I had gone to interview them about the operation of the Prevention of Terrorism Act, under which Irish people travelling between Britain and Ireland were liable to be detained without charge and questioned at length. These particular dockers had fallen foul of the legislation, having been detained at a port in England, and were recounting their experiences to me.

But when is there smoke without fire? Were these men perhaps involved in activities other than the loading and unloading of ships? Having heard their stories of arrest and alleged intimidation, I explained patiently to them the significance of those provisions of the law in the Republic of Ireland, known as 'Section 31', and asked each of them if he were a member of one of the proscribed organizations. As I included not only loyalist groups but also the IRA and Sinn Féin on my list, at least I got them to laugh. They denied being members or spokespersons of any of the listed bodies. Never! So that was alright then? No, of course it was not. They might have been lying. But I was covering my back to an extent as I intended to include some of the interviews in the programme that I was making. RTÉ might still unwittingly break the law when it transmitted my interviews if it turned out that any of the people included was in fact associated with one of the organizations against which the current Section 31 Statutory Order was aimed. I had no way of being certain that someone whom I interviewed had not previously been convicted of certain charges, or been otherwise openly associated in the past with particular organizations. Such a fact might have been reported in some Belfast newspaper, at some time, or be widely known in a local community. This could easily be the case, and the risk of missing something was even greater for a reporter based in Dublin, such as myself, than it was for one based in Northern Ireland. You could be sure that there were listeners or viewers out there, with their own political agendas and contacts, who would know or find out and who would not be slow to complain about my ignorance and about RTÉ's breach of Section 31. Then, some RTÉ editor would turn to me as the RTÉ reporter involved and I could plead that at least I had asked the particular interviewees about their possible membership of the proscribed organizations. Even exhaustive research in the form of lengthy background checks could never be exhaustive enough to preclude the possibility of error.

Considerations such as those just outlined had a chilling effect on the inclination of individual broadcasters to make programmes or reports dealing with controversies in Northern Ireland, or dealing with cross-border issues that might otherwise have included the participation of a member of one of the banned organizations. Moreover, what professional wants to do less than what he or she believes is required? No good journalist is happy to exclude material that ought to be in a story. Avoiding trouble by excluding actual or possible members of proscribed organizations was deeply unsatisfactory in circumstances where one felt that their contribution would add to the quality of any particular story. In any event, who wants to have to explain to dockers the niceties of Irish censorship law and to leave oneself open to charges that as a reporter 'you should have known' that a certain interviewee was a member of a certain organisation?

There were a number of options for any journalist coping with the restrictions imposed under Section 31. As already indicated, you could avoid stories about Northern Ireland altogether. This happened frequently in the case of journalists who were not actually assigned to work there. Or you could make stories about only certain aspects of society and politics in Northern Ireland, where you did not see a need to include people who might be considered spokespeople for particular organizations. This happened too, and it meant that whatever was going on inside poor and working-class communities, was even more inadequately reported than otherwise. Perhaps 'The Troubles' would never have become as bad as they did eventually had certain frustrations and injustices been openly reported and faced sooner. In such circumstances, an unhappy reporter might also convince her or himself that certain interviews were 'not really necessary'. This is a formula of words of which young journalists should beware. When an editor asks, 'Is that really necessary?' it too often means, 'For God's sake go and find some other way to tell the story that does not make trouble for me.' One can internalize that attitude and begin to steer clear of circumstances that mitigate against an easy life for oneself. At the end of the day, what is ever 'really necessary'? The appropriate response to the question is another question, 'What will really make the best report?'

COMPLIANCE VERSUS RESISTANCE

Given that Section 31 could be frustrating and awkward for journalists, it is fair to ask why there was not more opposition to it from working journalists and producers within RTÉ. Why did individuals such as myself not break it deliberately by including banned interviews in transmitted reports? I think that the answer is substantially threefold. Firstly, there was massive political support across the spectrum for Section 31. Secondly, there were many workers in RTÉ who saw no great harm in the provision, as well as some who even actively approved of it in practice. Thirdly, if you did break it then RTÉ, your employer, would have no choice in practice but to sack you for having broken the law. Few people relish the prospect of losing their job.

Each of the three reasons that I have given for the failure of workers within RTÉ to oppose Section 31 more vigorously is worth further consideration. In relation to the level of political support for Section 31 outside RTÉ, it ought to be remembered that a statutory instrument had to be laid before the Oireachtas annually renewing the list of proscribed organizations. At that point, each year, politicians had an opportunity to speak out against the provision. Few did so, and even those who did wasted little time on it because they recognised the broad level of support that it enjoyed. People who blame Section 31 on Conor Cruise O'Brien have a very simple view of its history. He had the intellectual courage to defend it, when others before or after him who were responsible for the broadcasting brief in cabinet and who maintained Section 31 were less assertive of its merits. O'Brien did not introduce the section and, in fact, amended it as the relevant Minister by insisting that the proscribing order must be specific and must be brought back to the Dáil every year to face possible rejection by the whole House.[1] The earlier row about the imprisonment of RTÉ's Kevin O'Kelly, and the sacking of an RTÉ Authority, had exposed at that time the undesirability of letting ministers have vague powers in relation to matters of freedom of expression, although it must be said that opposition to the continuation of such powers had never been sustained and widespread in Dáil Éireann.

It is hardly surprising to find that the sentiments of people working within RTÉ mirrored those of the politicians in Dáil Éireann when it came to paramilitary organizations and their political fronts. While the station and the trade unions objected occasionally to Section 31, many individuals were not particularly exercised about it. And some of those who were exercised about it appeared to be exercised in its favour. During my years at RTÉ, I became for a period what is known as 'The Father', or chairman, of the Programmes Chapel of the National Union of Journalists. I found no great appetite among its members, or indeed among the membership of another union representing many producers, for industrial action aimed at drawing public attention to the existence of the gagging order known as Section 31. Occasionally, there was a flutter of pickets, especially when journalists in Britain were objecting to the efforts there to impose a less restrictive but somewhat similar measure on United Kingdom broadcasters. Periodically, too, RTÉ newsreaders or reporters would announce on air that particular reports had been compiled under Section 31 restrictions. Some RTÉ programme-makers made minor protests by letting politicians know that they were not including them in a report because a spokesperson from some relevant but proscribed organisation could not also be included. But such measures were not consistently applied or maintained and never made much of an impact on the politicians or on the public.

As someone who always opposed Section 31, I found it quite frustrating that a number of journalists appeared to fear that by campaigning to repeal the provision they would be facilitating the work of men and women of violence. Cer-

---

1 See the chapter by Conor Cruise O'Brien, above.

tainly, any responsible journalist cannot but worry when providing a platform for the views of those who might subtly or not so subtly incite others to acts of violence. But I believe that the truth ultimately sets us free from error and delusion, and that it is better to hear all sides in a debate. At the same time, journalists ought not to lose sight of the need for robust questioning from a democratic perspective when interviewing the kinds of people against whom Section 31 was ostensibly intended to be aimed, namely those who will resort to violence as a matter of policy when persuasion fails and who readily ignore the democratically expressed wishes of the majority.

THE 'STICKIE' FACTOR IN RTÉ

I could at least understand the concerns of those colleagues in RTÉ who were worried, should journalists succeed in having the ban lifted, that their interviewing of members of the IRA and other organizations might somehow be turned by their interviewees into a means of inciting violence and mayhem. Indeed, given some of the weak interviewing of members of formerly proscribed organizations when Section 31 was later actually lifted, those worriers may have been right to be worried. However, what I found especially unpalatable was the manner in which a small number of RTÉ journalists and producers seemed quite content, in practice, to have Section 31 remain in force because it impacted most directly on 'The Provos'. These particular RTÉ employees were sympathetic to 'Official' Sinn Féin. The 'Provos', or 'Provisionals', were those sections of Sinn Féin and the IRA, which in December 1969, had split from the 'Officials' in an ideological dispute about tactics. The 'Officials' espoused an openly Marxist analysis of Irish society, north and south, and abandoned the long-standing Sinn Féin policy of electoral abstentionism. The 'Provisionals' believed that their former colleagues' interest in parliamentary politics had led to the movement's neglect of military matters and that this neglect had been vividly exposed during the disturbances of August 1969, when the IRA was not adequately prepared to defend Catholic areas of Northern Ireland against sectarian attacks. Those who remained in 'Official Sinn Féin', subsequently the Workers' Party, were known as 'Stickies' because the particular token distributed annually in return for a donation to one of their collectors on the street, was self-adhesive and did not require a pin like that of the old-fashioned and reactionary Provos. The 'Stickies' were active in RTÉ, and in other state-owned organizations, during the period in the late 1970s and early 1980s when I was employed by the station.

Members of the 'Stickies' in RTÉ were generally unhelpful to those who wished to see effective industrial action against Section 31, although some of them (and the party that they supported) occasionally expressed verbal opposition to Section 31 and admitted that its existence might falsify political debate. Those who were unhelpful in practice were neither the first nor the last to let their politics interfere with their professionalism. Notwithstanding a certain amount of socialist rhetoric, their views were not noticeably radical, and this was so particularly on issues such as Northern Ireland, industrialization and the environment. Their views often seemed quite indistinguishable from mainstream political opinion. For a while, they helped to create a broadcasting climate that was unfavourable to the calm consideration of strong nationalist sentiments. In this respect, they may have been well intentioned in that they wanted greater attention paid to the opinions of those on the island of Ireland who hold unionist opinions and who define themselves as British. They also played a useful role in focussing critical attention on any tendency on the part of media personnel in the Republic of Ireland to treat unionists as fundamentally unreasonable or wrong. However, the best antidote to such a tendency is fairness and balance, not some kind of remedial bias. In my opinion, one result of the ignoring of unpalatable nationalist sentiments was that RTÉ seemed ill-prepared to contextualize and interpret the level of support for the H-Block hunger strikes when Bobby Sands and his colleagues died in 1981.

A number of the supporters of the 'Stickies' in RTÉ benefited personally from the fact that they did not rock management's boat on Northern Ireland or on certain other issues. To put it another way, as I did some years ago, 'the ban has created a conservative climate which has impeded the progress of some journalists or producers with moderate nationalist views'.[2] The progress of people with moderate nationalist views would have been even more impeded had they taken it upon themselves individually to break the law and to transmit interviews prohibited under Section 31. This did not happen, with one somewhat ambiguous exception. In 1988, a reporter who contravened RTÉ management's interpretation of Section 31 did not have her contract renewed. The particular circumstances of Jenny McGeever's case as it unfolded muddled matters of principle with editorial, legal and industrial relations issues and never became a satisfactory cause around which the opponents of Section 31 might ultimately rally.[3]

CALLING THE SHOTS

McGeever was not the first broadcaster to fall foul of the provision, and an earlier case also illustrates the fact that governments would broach no ambiguity

---

2 Nally, D. 'The ban and toeing the line in RTÉ' in *Sunday Tribune*, 20 January 1991.   3 O'Meara, A. 'Journalists at odds as RTÉ faces unravelling of Section 31' in *Sunday Tribune*, 27 March 1988.

about their wishes in the matter. In 1982, a producer and presenter called Gavin Duffy had arranged for Gerry Adams and Danny Morrison of Sinn Féin to come to Dublin to take part in a discussion that was to involve also a live link-up with Ken Livingston of the Greater London Council. Duffy's programme was being made for Radio Leinster, an unlicensed or 'pirate' broadcaster that employed him. This was six years before the Oireachtas finally passed legislation to licence a range of radio and television stations other than the state-owned RTÉ, Ireland being one of the last states in western Europe to permit competition in broadcasting. At the time, regular transmissions by a number of 'pirates' were being tolerated by the state, partly to please younger voters by providing more popular music on the airwaves and partly to serve local communities with local news. When the Radio and Television Act of 1988 was later passed, it extended the provisions of Section 31 to all new licensed stations, but at the time of Gavin Duffy's programme the section only applied to RTÉ.

While it was an offence to broadcast without a licence, there had been no determined and sustained effort to shut down Radio Leinster or other pirates provided they did not interfere with frequencies used by emergency services or did not annoy authorities in the United Kingdom by deliberately attempting to attract audiences in that jurisdiction. However, the Irish authorities were alarmed when it became clear that Gavin Duffy intended to interview Gerry Adams and Danny Morrison. A letter from the Department of Posts and Telegraphs was delivered to the station by a messenger in a black Mercedes. The Department was reported to have warned Radio Leinster not to transmit its planned programme. The station's directors immediately cancelled the programme. Duffy stated publicly that he had seen the letter and that it warned that any such broadcast as that intended would be taken into account in deciding who might eventually be awarded licences to broadcast under future legislation. He claimed that his bosses wished to convince those whom they had described as 'the right people' that they intended to operate within the law as much as possible so that they might eventually get a licence.[4] The action by Radio Leinster served to remind those who supported or worked for unlicensed radio stations that these particular 'pirates' yearned for conformity and that their projection of a rebellious image was calculated to garner listeners rather than push out any boats when it came to current affairs. Employees like Gavin Duffy did not enjoy the potential support of large trade unions. However, employees of RTÉ did. So, why then, did RTÉ employees not take a stand on Section 31?

If RTÉ employees had swept aside both the shrinking violets and the 'Stickies' and had downed tools in protest, might a government of the day have decid-

4 Anon. 'Pirate radio producer sacked' in *Irish Times*, 24 December 1982.

ed against continuing its Section 31 provisions? Unions do not often decide to strike for matters of principle disconnected from their salaries or terms of employment. The consequences of their doing so in relation to Section 31 must remain an intriguing 'What if?' It is probable that any government would have seen such a strike as a direct challenge to its authority and would have been determined not to be seen to give in. Nevertheless, realistically, it might have been prepared to agree an interpretation of the annual statutory instrument that was less restrictive than that which operated within RTÉ. The agonising twists and turns of the policy of the National Union of Journalists towards Section 31 have been set out elsewhere, and that account indicates that a recurrent restraint on action was the fear that, if they silenced the airwaves in protest, its members could be accused of censorship themselves.[5]

The annual order under Section 31 directed RTÉ to 'refrain from broadcasting any matter which is an interview, or report of an interview, with a spokesman for any one or more of the following [named] organizations'. The word 'interview' was interpreted as meaning any recorded voice, even if it was that of a member of a listed organisation just reading a statement. Yet, the 'report of an interview' was not taken to exclude a broadcaster indirectly reporting a statement by a member of a listed organisation made to the general public. Any RTÉ employee who might be tempted to invite a member of one of the listed organizations to record a statement to the public solely for the sake of then quoting it was skating on thin ice. Nor was it ever considered possible to use the voices of actors in the mouths of proscribed persons being interviewed, as happened in Britain when somewhat similar legislation was introduced. This was because RTÉ considered such a ruse to constitute the reporting of an interview. And actors were out too when it came to reading statements. Why statements could be reported, but not carried when delivered by spokespeople or dubbed by actors, was never entirely clear, for it was only interviews and reports of interviews that were explicitly banned. In later years, the order was amended to include a specific prohibition on 'a broadcast by any person or persons representing ... Sinn Féin or the organisation styling itself Republican Sinn Féin'. This appeared to seal off the possibility, never utilized, of transmitting a recorded statement by these organizations. That this amendment referred only to two of the listed organizations was distinctly odd but reflected the political reality that the two organizations were thought to pose the greatest threat to the Irish state. The real possibility of their being entitled to airtime for party political broadcasts had arisen.

What might constitute a 'broadcast' by Sinn Féin raised some unforeseen issues. On one occasion I was covering an election count in Enniskillen, for RTÉ,

5 Horgan, J. 'Journalists and censorship: A case history of the NUJ in Ireland and the broadcasting ban, 1971-1994'. *Journalism Studies*, 3 (3) 2002, 377-92.

when Sinn Féin supporters began to chant one of their slogans in the background. The fact that we were live on air at the time possibly constituted a technical breach of Section 31 as it then stood. Another word in the annual Section 31 order that was certainly open to more than one interpretation was 'spokesman'. It was clear that this also included 'spokeswomen', in line with the normal interpretation of legislation. But it was not clear why it should include mere members, whether speaking about political or non-political matters. Yet, RTÉ interpreted it in that restrictive fashion. They seemed to feel that it could prove impossible in practice to know for certain whether or not a member of one of the organizations was acting as a spokesperson.

One other area where industrial action might have led to greater clarification was in respect of the sweeping provision that the ban extended to 'any organisation which in Northern Ireland is a proscribed organisation for the purposes of Section 21 of the Act of the British Parliament entitled the Northern Ireland (Emergency Provisions) Act, 1978'. The Oireachtas had written a blank cheque for the parliament of another jurisdiction (imprecisely referred to in the order as 'British' rather than that of the United Kingdom), and this was certainly unusual if not unique in the history of Irish censorship regulations. I recall asking the late John Kelly of Fine Gael, sometime Attorney General and author of a seminal text on the Irish Constitution, if he did not suspect that the latter part of the ban was unconstitutional. He answered that he did not, although it must be added that he himself supported Section 31.

RTÉ management believed that their conservative interpretation of the annual order conformed with the wishes of successive governments. The station took the view that discretion was the better part of valour in attempting to campaign against Section 31. Given that there was widespread political support for Section 31, management feared that a less restrictive interpretation might draw down the wrath of Dáil Éireann on the station's head and lead to the introduction of even harsher measures. As I wrote in *Fortnight* magazine in 1992, RTÉ management had been given to understand that the station was under threat from successive ministers: 'The threat was that if it did not read the government's intent accurately then it would face even more restrictive legislation.' The extent to which RTÉ remained very cautious even in the period immediately after the decision not to renew the Section 31 Order in 1994 was reflected in its newly updated guidelines for employees. These were more restrictive than those then circulated by the Independent Radio and Television Commission to non-RTÉ stations.[6]

6 MacCoille, C. 'How airwaves opened up for Sinn Féin' in *Sunday Tribune*, 23 January 1994; Connolly, F. 'Broadcasters oppose RTÉ guidelines' in *Sunday Business Post*, 6 February 1994; Kenny, C. 'Section 31 and the censorship of programmes' in *Irish Law Times and Solicitors' Journal*, n.s. xii (no. 3), March 1994, 50-52.

POLITICAL CENSORSHIP NOT SELF-CENSORSHIP

Some critics have seen evidence of what they call 'self-censorship' in RTÉ's con-
servatism, and especially in its willingness to appeal certain legal challenges to its
interpretation of Section 31, as well as in the failure of its employees to oppose
RTÉ's interpretation more robustly. While it is true that other interpretations of
the annual Order were theoretically possible, it is also the case that RTÉ lives in
a world of real politics and it is quite unrealistic to expect a publicly funded
broadcaster to defy aggressively what it perceives to be the broad political consensus on a matter of legal interpretation. To accuse RTÉ of self-censorship
seems to me to distract from the fact that Section 31 was a form of overt political censorship. It was censorship by the state, not self-censorship. RTÉ could
have done more to oppose Section 31, but neither RTÉ nor its employees were to
blame for its continuation.

In 1994, shortly before a government decided for strategic reasons not to renew
the annual order under Section 31, Michael McDowell, who later became Minister for Justice, argued in a newspaper article that Section 31 was 'not an issue of
censorship'. He added, 'It is not a question of the state trying to prevent us from
knowing what the Provos think.' He described the provision as 'simply a refusal by
the state to allow Sinn Féin access to the airwaves because Sinn Féin is not an ordinary political party but is an "integral part" of the IRA, as the Supreme Court
has found'.[7] His open and honest defence of Section 31, like that by Conor Cruise
O'Brien on other occasions, is useful in helping us to understand precisely why the
overwhelming majority of politicians long supported that provision. It was the
mainstream political establishment, not merely mavericks such as McDowell or
O'Brien, that piloted and maintained Section 31. Any demonisation of such individuals by opponents of Section 31 allows quieter, cuter or more cowardly members of Fianna Fáil, Fine Gael, Labour and the Progressive Democrats off the
hook of responsibility for the measure. On 25 May 1983, the Fianna Fáil leader,
Charles Haughey, described Section 31 as 'unnecessarily restrictive'; but within
hours his party's spokesman announced that this did not mean that Haughey
favoured lifting the ban in any way! Nor did he lift it, in practice.

The political censorship of Section 31 was effectively supported by all of the
major parties, albeit tempered by occasional expressions of reservation by individual politicians. They were probably terrified and enraged at the prospect of
seeing their own features mirrored on the television, reflected in the expressions
and words of spokesmen for Sinn Féin. Their own parties had long subscribed
to policies on Northern Ireland that were virtually indistinguishable in content
and rhetoric from those of Sinn Féin and the IRA. If they had softened their

7 McDowell, M. 'Section 31 is not an issue of censorship' in *Sunday Tribune*, 9 January 1994.

voices over the years, their words on paper still expressed old sentiments. So, they found it difficult to counter some of the passionate arguments of Sinn Féin, and they dreaded the emotions that these might inflame at times of crisis.

Beyond that, and for good reason, they regarded the IRA as a straightforward threat to the democratic authority of the Republic of Ireland. Most societies provide for limitations on the right of freedom of speech when the state is threatened, and political parties supported Section 31 in that context. It is easy to forget in times of peace, or in societies where there are no serious civil disturbances, just how fragile the social fabric can be when political emotions run high and violence breaks out. I remember on one particular occasion giving a guest lecture on 'Free Speech and the IRA: the Irish Dilemma' to students and staff at Simon Fraser University in Vancouver, British Columbia. The Irish experience was so far removed from that of western Canada that I sensed a complete failure on the part of the audience to grasp how democratic politicians might ever find it necessary to ban certain organizations from the airwaves. They had no concept of what all the fuss was for.

One thing that long irked broadcast journalists in Ireland, was the fact that Section 31 targeted only the airwaves. Journalists objected that if the IRA and other organizations such as Sinn Féin were a grave threat, then it was illogical to stop broadcasters from working with them while allowing their interviews to be carried by the print media and allowing some proscribed organizations that were not themselves overtly paramilitary to organise freely and to recruit new members. Sinn Féin, for example, was never banned and it has long published its own polemical paper. However, politicians were clearly convinced that the impact of speaking on radio and television was of a special magnitude. They were voting with their feet, and their statutory instruments, when it came to an assessment of media effects theory.

RISING TO THE CHALLENGE POST-SECTION 31

When the Oireachtas did decide, finally, to discontinue the annual banning orders under Section 31 and then to repeal the section itself, it did so *not* because it was converted anew to the principle of unfettered freedom of speech but because repealing Section 31 was a means of enticing Sinn Féin to participate in the 'peace process' and to sign up to the Good Friday Agreement. A measure that had been defended for years as a vital weapon in the armoury of the democratic state suddenly became a bargaining chip. Only when the electorates north and south were poised to vote in favour of a policy that embraced consent before unification, as they proceeded to do once referenda on the Good Friday Agreement were held, was it regarded as safe by most politicians to tamper with Section 31. If this attitude itself was politically inconsistent and not a matter of principle (if not unprincipled), there were not many journalists who were going to object. Now, broadcasters had what they had been looking for, which was an opportunity to exhibit their professionalism in the manner in which they interviewed members of organizations who had previously been banned from the airwaves.

There were immediate expressions of concern about how some broadcasters rose, or did not rise to that challenge. For example, Paddy Woodworth soon wrote that, 'This was the week in which all the nightmares of those who support Section 31 came true.'[8] Opinions still vary on the extent to which broadcast journalists have adequately questioned and reported on those people and organizations that were banned from the airwaves under Section 31.[9]

Today, the onus is on broadcasters to ensure that they apply the same professional criteria to interviewing members of the formerly proscribed organizations as they do to any other interviewee. The term 'professionalism' has been rightly interrogated by the political Left because it is sometimes used as a shield behind which class or sectoral interests hide or perpetuate unjustified privileges. But 'professionalism' can also be a badge of honour, worn by those who absorb the collective wisdom of generations of workers in a particular field. Those generations have deduced a method of responding appropriately to recurrent challenges or problems. One thing in particular that journalists learn is that just about everyone has something to 'sell', and that it is necessary to treat all interviewees with a certain scepticism if the truth is ever to come out. Allowing oneself to be overawed by ideological or paramilitary credentials is not a wise option for those who wish to be honest journalists rather than political acolytes.

Journalists aspire to the truth. From long before the moment that Pontius Pilate faced Christ and asked 'What is truth?',[10] thinkers in various cultures have speculated about that elusive concept or construct. That we continue to debate the matter implies that we believe that there are, at the very least, higher and lower levels of relative truth. It is a part of the job of journalists to aspire to the highest possible level. This should mean, for example, that a broadcaster does not permit paramilitary sympathizers to use radio or television to advance a series of complaints about the state unless the broadcaster also obliges them to face unpalatable facts about the organizations of which they themselves are members. This is so even if such facts are said by some to be 'unhelpful to the peace process', or even if the reporter senses an underlying danger that he or she may be punished for the persistent questioning of bullies by being denied access to an organisation's spokespeople in the future, or by more direct action.

8 Woodworth, P. 'Broadcasters fall into line as Adams calls the media tune' in *Irish Times*, 5 February 1994. Also see Drapier, 'Men of violence winning airwaves battle', in *Irish Times*, 9 April 1994.   9 See the chapter by Farrel Corcoran; below.   10 John 18:38.

Journalists face the daily challenge of negotiating media organizations and making professional judgments about what they perceive to be facts. While 'facts' are sacred, it is obvious that no two people may agree on what precisely are the most salient 'facts' to include in any particular media report. Journalists must swim in the sea, while others speculate about its ultimate nature. They negotiate treacherous waters, in which everyone from politicians to fashion models, and from media personnel to academics, are 'constructing' some interpretation of the facts. In this sea of relative subjectivity, journalists develop a practical appreciation of just how many degrees of truth there are. All have a better chance to show just how truthful and fair and professional they can be in the service of the general public since Section 31 ceased to operate as a mechanism of censorship.

6 / Government, public broadcasting and the urge to censor

FARREL CORCORAN

As many dissident artists have noted over the years, Irish society in the first half of the twentieth century tended to be closed and introverted, dominated by authoritarian traditions well entrenched in both church, state and many parts of civil society. Journalism too was influenced by the general cultural climate in which censorship thrived and it developed no great tradition of independence or assertiveness. The general tendency towards caution made it easier for political authorities to keep the media under control. So in the ten years before Section 31 was activated, it is not surprising to find that the urge to control broadcasting output was constantly bubbling under the political surface, though governments hesitated at the thought of actually invoking their legislative power to censor. It is worth reviewing the period of the 1960s briefly, to get a sense of this urge and the tensions that existed between government and the public broadcasting system it created.

THE URGE TO CENSOR

Shortly after Tom Hardiman became Director General in April 1968, the Chairman of RTÉ, Todd Andrews, invited the Minister in charge of Broadcasting, Erskine Childers, to dinner to meet the new chief executive of the country's most important cultural organisation. RTÉ had come through its first seven years of existence, the last three of them characterized by growing unhappiness among the staff at what was seen as increasing pressure from ministers to control television output in their favour. In the course of the meal, the Minister handed Andrews a plain sheet of paper containing about a dozen names of RTÉ employees and programme guests who, according to the Minister, were 'lefties, if not card carrying Communists, who should be treated as suspect subversives'. The Minister refused to disclose the source of the document, but Andrews immediately replied that it had been compiled by the Garda Special Branch (recently the object of a television documentary probe) under the inspiration of the 'paranoid Department of Justice', that RTÉ would pay no attention to the allegations, and that it was not the job of the Special Branch to 'institute a system of thought control or act as purveyors of political gossip'.[1] The Chairman made the point that as a young man he and many of his associates had suffered from harassment by the Special Branch, some being driven to emigration, and that he was determined that no one should suffer economically or otherwise for their political opinions. He later put these thoughts to the Minister in a letter and asked that it be shown to the Taoiseach, Seán Lemass. It wasn't, but secret lists were never mentioned again.

This dinner table vignette illustrates the enormous vulnerability of RTÉ to manipulation by the forces of the state. What is at stake is the demonstrated power of the media to shape the agenda of public discussion, to impose a primary definition on a controversy and to put a particular frame around issues of vital importance to the health of a democracy. RTÉ had to learn, through several bitter experiences, how to handle pressure from government and facilitate the emergence of an ethos that would have more in common with an ideal of public broadcasting rather than a state broadcasting model. Irish broadcasters and politicians had to learn, slowly and painfully, how to reconcile the desire for political freedom and the liberty of political choice, with the need to defend the cultural preconditions and accommodations on which both depend in the public sphere, especially freedom of expression.

There is no doubt that government found it extremely difficult to come to terms with the new radio and television organisation that it had created. Boundaries between government and RTÉ had to be established pragmatically, by experimentation and within the political culture of the time, each side testing its power and gauging possible reactions. Before the station opened, its first Director General, Ed Roth, asserted that RTÉ 'would not be a political organ of the government of the day'. After six long years of frustration, much of it with RTÉ's news and current affairs output, during which he dallied with the notion of establishing a Minister for Information to oversee the work of RTÉ, Lemass made his famous declaration in the Dáil that 'RTÉ was set up by legislation as an instrument of public policy and as such is responsible to the Government ... [T]o this extent the Government reject the view that RTÉ should be, either generally or in regard to its current affairs and news programmes, completely independent of Government supervision'.[2]

This well-prepared assertion of government power was prompted by a row between Charles Haughey, Minister for Agriculture, and the National Farmers Association, that dragged RTÉ – government tensions fully into the public spotlight. Haughey complained to the RTÉ newsroom about the insulting juxtaposition on the news of a statement from the NFA with a statement of his own. The NFA statement was deleted from subsequent bulletins. The NUJ and the

---

1 Andrews, C.S. (1982) *Man of no property*. Dublin: Mercier Press, 286.   2 Horgan, J. (1997) *Sean Lemass: the pragmatic patriot*. Dublin: Gill and Macmillan, 231.

Dublin newspapers were incensed by this interference. Haughey responded with further pressure on the current affairs television programme *Division*, which insisted on presenting both government and farmers' views. Haughey boycotted the programme but *Division* continued without Fianna Fáil input and its sister, the current affairs programme *Seven Days*, responded by devoting a whole week of programming to media freedom, exploring government and commercial interference in broadcasting in other European countries and the USA.[3]

Todd Andrews believed in the Lemass doctrine that it was the duty of the RTÉ Authority to support official policy and this emerged clearly in his handling of the Hanoi affair. The Authority initially supported the sending of a television team to North Vietnam in April 1967, feeling that RTÉ coverage of the war relied excessively on British and American sources, and that it was time that RTÉ developed a more ambitious news gathering operation in its coverage of world affairs. An Irish point of view could replace what was perceived as an excessive reliance on a British or American interpretation. When the Department of Foreign Affairs objected to this, Andrews' concern was to find out if the objection was based on a government decision or merely the personal view of an individual Minister. He considered, and then rejected, the possibility of insisting that if the government wanted the project cancelled, it should exercise its statutory powers of veto by issuing a formal instruction. He telephoned Jack Lynch, who had succeeded Seán Lemass as Taoiseach, and they agreed to publish a public statement to the effect that sending a news team to Hanoi 'would be an embarrassment to the Government in relation to its foreign policy'.[4] A short time later, a *Seven Days* team led by Muiris MacConghail, on its way to Biafra during the Nigerian civil war, was recalled when it was already in Lisbon, though Todd Andrews was at pains to point out to Garret FitzGerald at the time that the Irish Government was not involved in the decision. Despite this setback, a programme on Biafra was put together, combining acquired footage with an RTÉ commentary. This was criticized by the Nigerian Ambassador for giving 'an unfavourable and unfair impression of the Nigerian Government' and the Minister for Posts and Telegraphs asked the Authority for a copy of the programme. The uproar that ensued inside RTÉ, in the newspapers and in Dáil Éireann, focused on both inappropriate use of government power in broadcasting and excessive acquiescence to this power by RTÉ.

3 Doolan, L., Dowling, J. and Quinn, B. (1969) *Sit down and be counted: the cultural evolution of a television station*. Dublin: Wellington Publishers, 91.   4 Andrews, C.S., op. cit. 278.

THE EFFECTS ON RTÉ

Arising from these skirmishes, there were significant long-term consequences for the national broadcaster. Staff morale and confidence in senior management were left severely bruised. Many felt the Authority, which had been appointed to defend the rights of free expression in broadcasting, had abandoned those rights. Todd Andrews himself regretted not having insisted that the government use its statutory veto power, though this extended only to preventing the transmission of a programme, not gathering material for its production. Yet he and the Authority went on to veto a programme dealing with the activities of the Garda Special Branch, after it had been made and scheduled for transmission. The subsequent moving of *Seven Days* to the News Division, widely seen by staff as an expression of no confidence by the Authority in the Programmes Division, brought the organisation to the brink of an all-out strike.[5] Yet the government assumption throughout the 1960s, that it should control RTÉ as tightly as it could a government department, continued to impinge on the organisation and on public perceptions of the 'independence', or lack of it, in the national broadcasting organisation. When Director General, Kevin McCourt, resigned and the RTÉ Authority was in the process of selecting his successor, the Minister, Erskine Childers, conveyed the government's interest in knowing the names of applicants for the job, a request refused by Todd Andrews on the grounds of an obligation to observe confidentiality for all candidates.

The impact of Section 31 on RTÉ after 1972 has been well documented elsewhere (see especially Horgan, 2004 and other contributions in this volume), so only a few brief observations will be made here. Firstly, Section 31 acted as a censoring device in political communication for a long time but it can be argued that it also provided a form of protection for RTÉ in other areas. It allowed broadcasters to deflect inappropriate government pressure by pointing out that there was a statutory method available – the written directive – should government choose to use it. Both sides knew that government was unwilling, for political reasons, to invoke Section 31 except in the most serious circumstances. Secondly, Irish newspapers provided very little editorial support for RTÉ in its early difficulties with political censorship (though NUJ members supported their colleagues in RTÉ who used a 48-hour work stoppage to protest against Kevin O'Kelly's conviction in 1972). There is even some evidence that a 'Section 31 mindset' took a hold on newspapers too, though they of course had no legal obligations under the 1960 Act.[6] Thirdly, many of the more absurd applications of Section 31 (such as its extension to court reporting, or the cutting of two minutes

5 Doolan et al., op. cit. 102. 6 Doornaert, M. & Larsen, H. (1987) *Censoring the 'Troubles': an Irish solution to an Irish problem? Report of an IFJ fact-finding mission to Ireland, January 1987.* Brussels: International Federation of Journalists, 10-11.

from a Robert Kee documentary on Irish history purchased from ITV, or the censoring of Sinn Féin members' views on industrial relations disputes or rose-growing or bee-keeping) can be traced to the imprecise language in which directives were written and government refusal to offer clarification. The technique used by Kevin O'Kelly in his controversial 1972 radio programme, for instance - reporting on an interview with an IRA leader without allowing the leader's voice on air - was used by another journalist, Liam Hourican, a little while earlier and produced no adverse government reaction. (In the attempt to allow some information about the IRA to be transmitted, RTÉ reporters later resorted to the expedient of having one journalist interview another journalist who had interviewed an IRA member.) Fourthly, the history of RTÉ's adjustment to Section 31 directives is characterized by complex tensions between and within trade unions in broadcasting, and between the RTÉ branch and the NUJ headquarters. Tensions between the National Union of Journalists and the Workers' Union of Ireland were particularly strong and tended to amplify existing organizational turf wars between News (staffed mostly by NUJ members) and Current Affairs (staffed mostly by WUI members in the Programmes Division) over coverage of general elections, budgets and other critical events. Attempts to answer the rather innocent question of why RTÉ workers could not have found a consensus against accepting censorship, or in favour of constantly testing the limits of the regulations, must take this frequently fractious and bitter trade union history into account.

Many of the later criticisms of RTÉ's excessive caution in investigative journalism and its constant apprehensions about government attitudes in general, should be examined in the context of organizational reactions to a prolonged period of censorship. Editorial caution can be seen in hindsight as one of the long-term, deep structural effects of Section 31. A 1977 NUJ document, for example, notes that 'the ultra-cautious atmosphere which Section 31 and the guidelines have fostered in the newsroom and programme sections has meant that enquiries into controversial areas have not been encouraged ... There is now a general anxiety about tackling stories which might embarrass the government on the issue of security.'[7] Ten years later, an International Federation of Journalists fact-finding mission to Ireland to examine the question of news censorship pointed to several contradictions in the application of Section 31, including the banning of Sinn Féin from the airwaves but the official recognition of it as a legitimate political party. Several journalists and editors interviewed by the IFJ team saw Section 31 in the light of Irish Governments responding to British pressure, while at the same time gaining some electoral advantage at home in denying

---

7 Horgan, J. (2004) *Broadcasting and public life: RTÉ news and current affairs*. Dublin: Four Courts Press.

publicity to Sinn Féin. The IFJ concluded that 'the most dangerous effect of the present Section 31 practice is the creation of a general climate in which restrictions on the media and free journalism are accepted and defended'.[8]

POST-SECTION 31 ADJUSTMENTS

The Section 31 directive was finally allowed to lapse in January 1994 in the lead-in to establishing a new IRA cease-fire.[9] The British ban was lifted shortly afterwards. The Minister in charge of broadcasting, Michael D. Higgins, argued that 'deterministic' views of television's power over viewers were now outdated and that people had the capacity to make up their own minds about what they saw on television. The final act in the long saga of Section 31 was RTÉ's own difficult adjustment to the new censorship-free environment. This writer found himself at the centre of this period of change, as a participant rather than an observer, when he was appointed Chairman of the RTÉ Authority for the period from 1995 to 2000.

Passionate debate was the order of the day when we came to discuss how RTÉ journalists were handling Sinn Féin interviews, in a broadcasting atmosphere adapting very cautiously to the ending of the ban. In the opinion of many commentators, but probably not a majority on the RTÉ Authority, the decisive ministerial action of allowing the Section 31 directive to lapse, reversing a policy that had been in place for two decades, was to play a major role in advancing the peace process in Northern Ireland. I believe historical hindsight will validate this judgment. But in the first few years of post-Section 31 broadcasting, I could never be sure that a majority of my colleagues didn't deeply resent the newfound freedom of Sinn Féin to speak directly to journalists and to Irish audiences. Over the previous two decades, many complex layers of self-censorship regarding 'The Troubles' had evolved within RTÉ, aided by the formation of unofficial staff watchdog groups associated with Sinn Féin the Workers' Party, which had descended directly from Official Sinn Féin after the split in the Republican movement in the early 1970s. The 'Stickies', as they were popularly known, had become increasingly sympathetic to unionist and revisionist interpretations of the conflict in Northern Ireland and pushed their newfound interpretation of the conflict through the Ned Stapleton Cumann, which operated within the RTÉ branch of the Workers' Union of Ireland. Pressures towards censorship, deeply embedded in different parts of the organisation, intimidated staff into accepting, however reluctantly, forms of self-censorship that went far beyond the letter of Section 31. President Mary McAleese has given some insight into the editorial atmosphere

8 Doornaert, M. et al., op. cit., 18.   9 The order lapsed on 19 January 1994.

of her time in RTÉ, sometimes encountering a tendency towards anti-nationalist bullying in her work as a researcher in Current Affairs, especially around the
time when hunger striker Bobby Sands was elected to parliament at Westminster
in the early 1980s.[10] Revisionism had also taken a grip on most of the national
newspapers, to the extent that many print journalists avoided important stories
like the Guilford Four and the Birmingham Six miscarriages of justice, for fear
of being labelled Provo sympathisers.

The challenge in 1996 was how to sweep away the damaging aftermath of the
censorious mindset of the 'Stickies' and remove the fear of being a 'hush puppy'
(the derogatory term used to signify those considered to be 'soft' on the Provisional IRA and Sinn Féin). The challenge was made all the more difficult because
of the deeply coded way in which discussion of this problem usually took place
within RTÉ, even at senior management level. It was difficult for a newcomer like
myself to decode some of the talk, and some of the silences, about the internal
censorship campaign waged by the 'Stickies'. In some cases, there were obvious
similarities with the anti-communism hysteria and the purges of staff in the US
media industry in the early 1950s, where various layers of guilt for not recognising and resisting the danger to free speech represented by McCarthy outlasted the
end of the actual purges by several years.

The question of how to handle Sinn Féin, newly released from years of broadcasting exile, surfaced in Authority discussions in 1996, initially in the form of
reactions to news coverage of anti-drugs campaigns in Dublin's inner-city neighbourhoods and Sinn Féin's role in them. There is a certain irony in the fact that
as journalists were adjusting slowly to the ending of Section 31 censorship, RTÉ
was at the same time working to increase its transmission power northwards. This
reflected the belief that by achieving symmetry of television reception on both
sides of the border RTÉ could play a role in increasing mutual understanding
between unionist and nationalist cultures and perhaps achieving reconciliation
across the various borders of tradition, politics, religion, group memory and historical identity that had plagued Ireland for so long. RTÉ engaged in diplomat-
ic negotiations and engineering field strength trials that precede full-power oper-
ations in a very low-key manner, announcing the increased television availability
in the North only to television set dealers and on teletext. This was to avoid
adverse reaction and xenophobic outbursts from politicians representing certain
sections of Northern Ireland society who would abhor the ideological pollution
that would start drenching the population from full-power RTÉ transmitters,
now liberated from Section 31.

The summer marching season in Northern Ireland presented special challenges to the Newsroom. How does a journalist maintain high standards of fair-

10 Mac Manais, R. (2003) *Maire Mac Giolla Iosa: Breathaisneis.* Galway: Chló Iar-Chonnachta.

ness, impartiality and objectivity in some of the highly-charged, key confrontations in the summer calendar, where one group is driven by fanatical feelings of group superiority, historically rooted in the need to intimidate neighbours, and another group is organising resistance to this triumphalism? There was a certain timidity on the part of the RTÉ Newsroom about coverage of the Northern Ireland summer confrontations over use of public space for marching, a fear that television news, as it sought to report on events, might in fact inflame those events. This was the old Yeatsian worry that our words and our pictures might send certain young men out to die. My academic instinct was to distrust this 'hypodermic' paradigm of media effects – the notion of media directly, powerfully and uniformly influencing viewers – as a simplistic approach to understanding the television viewing experience, already abandoned by media theorists.[11] Whatever about a poet's verse, television output has an impact that is more inclined to be indirect, complex and biased towards cultivating a 'mainstream' view.

Some Authority colleagues worried about Charlie Bird's animated style of delivery, in his reports from northern hotspots like Drumcree and the Apprentice Boys march in Derry.[12] My fear was that an institutional timidity about reporting Northern Ireland, deeply entrenched in Section 31-induced self-censorship patterns, might continue to produce a televisual blandness that would bore and alienate audiences and lack relevance, rather than grip and involve the core RTÉ audience. If it is to remain relevant to Irish people, RTÉ must in fact be shielded from all forms of censorship, so that it can sharpen its critical edge. The colour and emotion in Charlie Bird's reports were therefore to be valued for the way in which a real sense of the tensions in Northern Ireland could be communicated to people who rarely travel north of the border. After all, within a few years, new commercial radio and television stations would be reporting in their own graphic styles, unencumbered by any institutional memory of 'Stickies' or Section 31.

THE SINN FÉIN CHALLENGE

Such was the unhealthy legacy of Section 31 in RTÉ that loose talk about 'robust journalism' could be quickly recoded as 'hush puppy journalism' that might give succour to the Provos. Some colleagues on the Authority believed that the RTÉ newsroom had a 'Republican agenda' and that this was obvious in its coverage of the anti-drugs campaigns in Dublin, which did not sufficiently highlight the 'sinister' leadership role of Sinn Féin in these inner-city crusades against drug deal-

11 See the chapter by Mary P. Corcoran, below.   12 Then RTÉ's chief news correspondent.

ers. But side by side with this view on the Authority was the criticism that some RTÉ programmes were treating Sinn Féin politicians in an unnecessarily aggressive way. The phenomenon of selective perception operated consistently in this area, linking commentators' personal orientations to 'The Troubles' with their perceptions of how RTÉ was handling Sinn Féin. In the jargon of the time, who was in charge of the news, 'Stickies' or 'Shinners'? The question was something of a Rorschach test.

In 1997, Authority discussions about Sinn Féin tended to focus on two questions: was Sinn Féin being given too much access on the airwaves and were RTÉ staff adequately prepared in interviews to manage the very considerable oratorical acumen believed to reside within the Sinn Féin organization? Some colleagues felt RTÉ needed clearer editorial guidelines as to when it was appropriate to interview a Sinn Féin spokesperson, as the party was adroit in managing its media exposure to suit its own circumstances. We tended to disagree over whether there was too great a presence of Sinn Féin people on air. On the one hand, the party was relatively small in electoral terms and its share of broadcast time should arithmetically reflect this. On the other, decisions made by Sinn Féin were inherently more newsworthy than the moves of most other parties, since they were the main conduit of information from the IRA about maintaining a ceasefire, and later, moving towards decommissioning weapons, two key aspects of the unfolding drama of the peace process.

There was by now no longer a strong belief among members of the Authority that there was a seriously sympathetic ethos in favour of Sinn Féin embedded among RTÉ staff, and certainly no fear of a conspiracy to promote its aims in contravention of the legal requirement for RTÉ to observe impartiality in its news and current affairs output. Eoghan Harris, long since retired from RTÉ, stridently kept alive his 'hush puppy' accusations from the vantage point of a weekly column in the *Sunday Times*, but the actual debate had moved on to the notion that RTÉ staff were simply not able to handle the very sophisticated debating skills of people like Gerry Adams, Martin McGuinness and Mitchell McLoughlin. RTÉ managers were frustrated by Sinn Féin's capacity not to respond to critical questions posed by journalists, or to respond only with bland truisms, particularly when challenged to clarify the Party's relationship with the IRA. This was an obsessive question, on the lips of most journalists in 1998, and Sinn Féin was giving coy or evasive answers when challenged, or brilliant long-winded lectures on nationalist history. The ambiguity inherent in Sinn Féin's depiction of its relationship with the IRA was intensely frustrating for many journalists, though commentators today would tend to acknowledge the necessary role played by ambiguity on all sides in this period, in keeping the peace process alive for so long. Most broadcast interviews quickly turned into very emotionally tense debates, and the concern about this at Authority and senior management levels tended to be framed in terms of perceived imbalances in debating skills: on the one side, naive and poorly trained RTÉ journalists, and on the other, battle-hardened men and women whose debating prowess stemmed from long years of training in survival skills, including, as we were reminded by one Authority colleague, preparation for the intense experience of interrogation in grim RUC and British Army conditions, far removed from the niceties of Dublin 4 studios.

To my mind, the bottom line for the Authority was to avoid a situation where a heavy-handed top-down regime of managerial control would be re-imposed on journalists before they had the time to get to grips with Sinn Féin's debating style. It was vital to avoid the re-imposition of the rules of upward-referral put in place in the Newsroom in the immediate aftermath of the suspension of Section 31 but then relaxed. Even a partial re-imposition of censorship would be no help to the peace process. There was certainly an imbalance in many interviews on radio and television in this period, where RTÉ journalists seemed frequently to be losing the argument. Even the urbane Gay Byrne, who had interviewed kings, emperors and vagabonds with supreme confidence, seemed to some critics to come off second best in his very wary encounter with Gerry Adams on the *Late Late Show*.

Any realistic analysis of the situation would have to conclude that Gerry Adams and Martin McGuinness were not at this time going to clarify the exact nature of their relationship with the IRA, no matter how high the 'skill levels' of RTÉ journalists. When they were allowed access to the airwaves from 1994 on, it was inevitable that they would have long, pent-up tales to tell of oppression and humiliation suffered by the nationalist population in Northern Ireland over many decades, whether or not we in the Republic wanted to listen. Sinn Féin had been waiting a long time to tell its side of a story. Hitherto, the story had been dominated for a very long time by the press relations skills of the British army, aided by friends in the London newspaper establishment like the *Daily Telegraph*.[13] But RTÉ had been conditioned by decades of censorship to be unprepared for these outpourings, which were radically transforming the mix of political information available to Irish citizens. At no time was I sure that a majority of my colleagues on the Authority agreed with me, some claiming that they knew what was 'really going on' inside what was called 'Sinn Féin-IRA'. The problem was never formally put on the agenda for an Authority meeting and it was never voted on. My tendency was to put the brakes on discussions that took the form of circling back

13 Miller, D. (1994) *Don't mention the war.* London: Pluto Press; Miller, D. (1994) *Rethinking Northern Ireland: culture, ideology and colonialism.* London: Longman; Rolston, B. (1996) *War and words: the Northern Ireland media reader.* Belfast: Beyond the Pale Publications; Curtis, L. (2000) *Ireland: the propaganda war.* Belfast: Sasta; Fennell, D. (1993) *Heresy: the battle of ideas in modern Ireland.* Belfast: Blackstaff Press.

towards the comfort zone of the old Section 31 mentality. We compromised on a stance of light-touch supervision by the Director General in this sensitive and contentious area, and avoided re-imposing upward-referral rules about contact with Sinn Féin.

It was important not to let these teething difficulties in the initial stages of the post-Section 31 era force us to decide prematurely on another very long-running question: should Television News and Current Affairs maintain their editorial separateness, or should they be organizationally merged, forming one structural entity where the 'rashness' of reportorial impulses to chase the immediate story might be tempered by the more reflective and analytical instincts of Current Affairs? Such a hasty decision on our part might in fact have been counterproductive, in the sense of signalling that we expected Current Affairs to play the 'safe' role. All of our discussions on the future of Current Affairs in fact were critical of the voices of caution that envisaged Current Affairs as essentially the location for the elaboration of stories broken elsewhere in the Irish media. We were unanimous in urging Current Affairs to listen to the accusations of blandness and timidity levelled at RTÉ by its more intelligent critics, to invest resources in investigative journalism and to trust the Authority to be supportive when good journalistic work was accomplished, even if that might sometimes disturb political authorities and other vested interests in Irish society.

The shadow of Section 31 still fell over RTÉ at the beginning of 1998 (four years after it had ceased to have legal power) when the Secretary of State for Northern Ireland, Mo Mowlam, decided to visit Republican and Loyalist prisoners in jail, to engage with their views on the peace process. Rules for allowing the views of paramilitaries to be broadcast were broken in at least one instance (an unauthorized interview with a UFF prisoner in the Maze prison, aired on *Today with Pat Kenny*) and were soon relaxed. But it is significant that what exercised minds in RTÉ at this time was not the intermittent airing of convicted prisoners' views but the daily challenge of dealing with Sinn Féin as it moved inexorably towards the centre of mainstream politics and the signing of the Good Friday Agreement.

CONCLUSION

Final considerations in this chapter must return to the question of the relationship between government and public broadcasters, whose programme output occupies a special place in public discourse. But one dimension of this special status is that it makes public broadcasting particularly vulnerable to the political urge to censor. This is not a uniquely Irish problem, as we can see from recent events in England and Italy. The Hutton Inquiry was established in London in the second half of 2003 to investigate the role of the BBC and the British government in conveying to the public, information about the level of threat posed by Saddam Hussein's regime in Iraq. It brought government-broadcaster tensions to new levels of intensity. Until Hutton, 2003 had been a very good year for the BBC. The New Labour government had appointed one of Tony Blair's advisors on broadcasting policy (author of the Davies Report on the BBC) to be Chairman and had promised a major role for the BBC in the roll out of digital television, after the collapse of private sector efforts in Digital Terrestrial Television. Its Freesat digital system was destined to take the Corporation to new heights of success even beyond the borders of the UK. But all this depends ultimately on the continued goodwill of the British government. Even before the Gilligan / Campbell clash which lead to the Hutton Inquiry, many in New Labour were asking, is the BBC not biting the hand that feeds it, in a most public and embarrassing way, through its news coverage of Iraq? The devastating findings of the Hutton Report, which exonerated the government and blamed the BBC for editorial and reporting shortcomings in its coverage of the war, resulted in the resignation of both the Chairman and Director General. The BBC has been badly shaken and it remains to be seen how these two major British institutions, government and public broadcaster, will relate to each other in the future.

In other countries, governments lean towards the view that private television companies can be trusted to be more supine than public broadcasters when it comes to the watchdog role of the media. Hostile newspapers are not to be taken lightly at election time, but hostile television channels are too much to tolerate. In Italy, Prime Minister Silvio Berlusconi now exercises unprecedented power over both the public and the private television systems. His control over the public broadcasting system RAI has tightened to the point where major broadcasting trade unions are objecting to sinister forms of 'manipulation' of RAI news output and documenting it all in a 'White Book', while many critics believe RAI news is being deliberately turned into a distraction rather than a credible source of information. The Italian government is poised, early in 2004, to privatize parts of the RAI system.

In Ireland, Ray Burke, Minister for Communication in the early 1990s, had a devastatingly negative impact on public service broadcasting and this alerted many people to the dangers that can arise when political power is abused. Could RTÉ be damaged in the future by massive political influence? Will its structures of regulation and governance, once the new Broadcasting Act is passed, always pass the Berlusconi test? In order to ensure that government will not react aggressively against it in the future, will RTÉ always be able to follow its editorial, rather than its political instincts, when it is timely to critique government performance? In a much more competitive broadcasting environment, will RTÉ be able to project the 'whiff of danger' that audiences increasingly want, particularly when it turns its cameras on the politics of corporate Ireland? There has been one positive development in recent years: the changes brought about by the Freedom of Information Act 1997. One of the main reasons for the decline in overt pressure on broadcasters from powerful interests in political institutions is the knowledge that what may be intended as a quiet word in the ear of the Chairman or the Director General may well end up on the front page of a newspaper or in a feature story in a current affairs television programme. The very real possibility of publicity is itself one of the principal bulwarks against interference.

7 / Censorship and 'The Troubles'

ED MOLONEY

Amid the panoply of counter insurgency weapons employed by the British and Irish states during 'The Troubles' in Northern Ireland, the use of media censorship is rarely mentioned or assigned the importance that it deserves. One reason for this, quite possibly, is that most accounts of the conflict to date have been written by journalists who, understandably, are not yet willing to acknowledge that censorship played such a large role in shaping the media's coverage of events. Or it may be that the authorities in London or Dublin are not particularly keen to flaunt their use of a tactic regarded by their democratic allies as a hallmark of totalitarian regimes and thus deserving of condemnation.

But media censorship was a consistent and key feature of the way both states dealt with 'The Troubles' almost from the outset of violence in 1970 — and it has survived into the peace process where those who were once its victims are now amongst its keenest practitioners. Like other tactics deployed in the subsequent quarter of a century or so, media censorship evolved and changed, taking different forms in each state at different times, according to the needs and limitations of the day. Formal, or legalized censorship enforced by law in both jurisdictions and directed principally against the electronic media was its most dramatic and visible manifestation. But alongside it, intangible but arguably as, if not more effective, was its informal manifestation, self-censorship, which can be defined as the journalistic practice of voluntarily suppressing a story, or an angle on a story, for fear of the damage that doing otherwise would have on an individual's career trajectory. These two forms of censorship existed side by side and sustained each other in significant ways. Formal censorship encouraged self-censorship which in turn spread from the electronic to the print media, where official censorship did not apply and by so doing discouraged any challenge to formal censorship. A vicious, self-sustaining circle had been created.

The other defining feature of censorship was that its principal target was violent, physical force republicanism, especially the Provisional IRA and its political wing, Sinn Féin. Loyalist paramilitary groups were included in the lists of bodies banned from the airwaves, but it was the challenge to both states from the IRA that brought censorship into being and sustained it. Only when the threat of violence from the IRA receded was formal censorship ended.

A DELICATE DEMOCRACY

Of the two states, the Irish state was the more threatened when the IRA began its campaign of defensive and then offensive violence in 1970, and it was the Irish state that first resorted to formal censorship. There were particular reasons for this. The Provisionals had emerged from a civil rights movement that had highlighted discrimination and violence directed at the Catholic community by the ruling Unionists and this had generated considerable sympathy and support amongst co-religionists in the South which, if anything, mushroomed when the British army, cheered on by the Unionist government, turned against the Catholics they had been sent to protect. The outpouring of public anger after Bloody Sunday in January 1972, culminating in the burning of the British embassy in Dublin, was eloquent testimony to that.

The twenty-six county state was also fragile. Less than fifty years old when 'The Troubles' began, it had been forged in violent conflict between the IRA and the British military, exactly the same combatants battling it out on the streets of Belfast and Derry in the early 1970s. Far from being regarded as an alien, terrorist menace, the IRA was as much part of Irish culture as Catholicism or the GAA. Furthermore, the scars of the civil war that had followed British disengagement from the South, and a settlement bitterly opposed by hard-line Republicans, were still raw. In the minds of many, the eruption of violence in the North was an opportunity to complete the unfinished business of 1921. The South was, at the outset of 'The Troubles', potentially fertile ground for the burgeoning Provisional IRA and vulnerable.

If the Irish democracy was still delicate by the time 'The Troubles' started, few of its institutions had been as tested as had the media. Media censorship had been routinely practised over the years by the British to suppress movements for Irish independence and during the 1919–1921 Anglo-Irish conflict, the Defence of the Realm Act, passed at the outbreak of European hostilities in 1914, gave the authorities sweeping powers to ban newspapers and imprison journalists suspected of harbouring IRA sympathies. Following the formation of the Irish Free State, the new government was as keen to control the media as the British had been, not just to curb opponents of the Treaty but to protect the Catholic ethos of the new state and to resist the cultural intrusion of England and America. In 1926 the government sought to regulate the print and publishing media through the 'Committee on Evil Literature' and three years later established the Irish Censorship Board that had sweeping powers to ban books and periodicals that offended Catholic doctrine on issues like contraception. The powers also applied to films, and between 1923 and 1970 some 1000 movies were banned and 10,000 altered and cut. It was against this background that in 1960 the publicly owned

Irish broadcasting system was reorganised and placed under the control of a new agency, Radio Telifís Éireann (RTÉ). Television broadcasts began a year later and by 1966, the then Taoiseach Seán Lemass, a veteran of the IRA's 1919–1921 campaign for independence and now leader of Fianna Fáil, was making it clear that he regarded RTÉ as just another arm of government. The public broadcasting service, he declared, could not be independent of government supervision and was 'an instrument of public policy' as much as any department of state.[1] The next few years saw a series of public and private battles between the government and RTÉ management over both the content of programmes that the government found objectionable and the treatment of ministers by RTÉ journalists during interviews.

TIGHTENING THE SCREW

By the time the Northern violence erupted there was a track record of meddling in RTÉ's affairs and a history of state interference in the other media. Not surprisingly there was little opposition when in October 1971 the government issued an Order under Section 31 of the Broadcasting Act banning the transmission of items that 'could be calculated to promote the aims or activities of any organization which engages in, promotes, encourages or advocates the attaining of any particular objectives by violent means'.[2] The wording was vague and general but the meaning became clear thirteen months later when RTÉ broadcast a report of an interview with the then IRA Chief of Staff, Sean MacStiofain. MacStiofain was arrested and jailed as was the journalist who had interviewed him, Kevin O'Kelly while the entire RTÉ Authority, the body charged with governing the station, was sacked. The first move made by the government against broadcasters to control coverage of the Northern conflict was a repressive one.

A year later the censorship screw was tightened when a Fine Gael-Labour coalition took office and Conor Cruise O'Brien became Minister for Posts and Telegraphs with oversight of RTÉ. Defying an international reputation as a liberal scholar, O'Brien left office four years later with his name now a byword for savage censorship. 'The Cruiser', as he was known, regularized Section 31 and specified by name the organizations whose spokespersons or members were banned from the airwaves. The list included not just the IRA but also its political wing, Sinn Féin, which was legal and public. At an informal level he launched an unprecedented campaign of intimidation against journalists, for example labelling those he regarded as soft on the IRA as 'Provo stooges' and letting it be

1 Purcell, B. 'The silence in Irish broadcasting' in Rolston, B. (ed.) (1991) *The media and Northern Ireland: covering the Troubles*. London: Macmillan, 51–69 at 54. 2 Purcell, B., op. cit.

known that he was compiling a file of allegedly subversive letters published in the *Irish Press* newspaper.[3]

The effect of O'Brien's campaign was felt at two levels. Terrified at the consequences of angering O'Brien and his colleagues, RTÉ's coverage of 'The Troubles' became characterized by timidity and an adherence to a presentation of events in the North in which condemnation of violence rather than an explanation for its existence and persistence became the guiding principle of programme-makers. Controversial issues, such as human rights abuses that served to fuel the conflict, were mostly ignored on the grounds that they could be misused as propaganda for the IRA or, if they were covered, were filtered through an agenda-cluttered prism. Investigative journalism gave way to a chary – and dull – recitation of on-the-record events. The primary duty of journalism, to explain, to elucidate, to expose and to hold the institutions of society to account was significantly eroded.

RTÉ journalists became ultra cautious about all the programmes they made, opting to drop items if there was a remote possibility that they might interview a member of Sinn Féin, even inadvertently and even if the programme had nothing to do with 'The Troubles'. Examples of Section 31 in action in this way were sometimes ludicrous, such as the banning of a caller to RTÉ's gardening radio programme who declared himself to be a Sinn Féin member. But more serious stories with no connection at all to the conflict in the North also suffered. A list of programmes in this category that were banned or censored compiled by RTÉ producer Betty Purcell included items as diverse as a grassroots campaign against drug-dealers in Dublin because Republicans were said to be involved, the sacking of a single pregnant teacher by her Catholic nun employers because the father of her child was said to be in Sinn Féin, an AIDS awareness programme because its spokesman was also in Sinn Féin, clashes in Dublin between street traders and police because one of those arrested was a Sinn Féin politician and numerous housing problems in Dublin because some of those at demonstrations could be Republicans. The slightest suggestion that a Sinn Féin voice might be broadcast on RTÉ was enough to persuade management at the station to drop the item. Journalists at the station, unbidden, chose to interpret Section 31 in the harshest, widest way. 'Whole neighbourhoods of people were silenced because they [were] too close to the possibility of breaking the ban. The question [was] not, "Who is in Sinn Féin?" but, "Who is definitely *not* in Sinn Féin?" wrote Purcell.[4]

At another level, O'Brien's campaign launched a McCarthyite wave of fear that engulfed journalists at RTÉ. The fear was a simple but chilling one: to suggest making controversial and challenging programmes on the North or even to

---

3 See the chapter by Mark O'Brien, above.   4 Purcell, B. ,op. cit., 61.

express opposition to Section 31 and censorship was to invite an accusation of sympathy and support for the IRA and its violent methods. An allegation like that was enough to end or side-track a promising career and reporters and editors soon learned that the surest way to keep their jobs was to steer clear of the North or to tread with extreme caution when dealing with it, a theme explored elsewhere in this volume.

The situation in RTÉ during the late 1970s and 1980s was worsened by the disproportionate influence exerted over the station's news and current affairs division by the Workers' Party, some of whose members held key production and editorial posts there. The Workers' Party were the descendants of that section of the IRA that split away from the Provisionals at the start of 'The Troubles'. Bitter opponents of the Provos and their nationalist ideology, the Workers' Party was a hardline, Stalinist organization, fiercely loyal to the politics and practices of the Soviet Union and dedicated to a tactic of infiltrating trade unions and public bodies like RTÉ. Presented with the opportunity to do damage to their former colleagues in the Provisionals, Workers' Party journalists at RTÉ enforced Section 31 with gusto and enthusiasm, presiding over what many RTÉ journalists would privately describe as a reign of terror. Conor Cruise O'Brien may have promulgated the censorship of RTÉ, but its political commissars came from in-house.

THE DIFFUSION OF A CENSORSHIP CULTURE

Formal, government-directed censorship of RTÉ and informal, self-censorship within RTÉ soon spilled over into the print media, a process accelerated by the smallness of the Irish media and the dominant role played in the affairs of the Irish state in those days by the national broadcaster. The same timidity and fear that characterized RTÉ's coverage of the North soon infected Ireland's newspapers and it worked in a remarkably similar fashion. The author, who was a reporter both in *Hibernia* magazine and in the Belfast office of the *Irish Times* during some of the most intense years of censorship – the late 1970s and early 1980s – had personal experience of the mechanics of this process. It worked like this: if you suggested a story, say on the authorities' use of uncorroborated evidence from IRA supergrasses during terrorist trials – a controversial security tactic that had serious implications for the judicial process – then the assumption was made that to do so, you must have been in touch with IRA people or types very close to them. Since that must also mean that you had talked to them, possibly at some length, and since decent, respectable journalists who abhorred violence would never do that, the conclusion was that either you got on with IRA figures and liked them or even that you sympathised with them. In either case you had got far too close to the men of violence and had become suspect. It was often be the same for other stories such as the 1982 shoot-to-kill incidents, the framing of the Birmingham Six and the Guildford Four, allegations of police brutality at Castlereagh, deteriorating prison conditions in the H-Blocks and so on – in fact any story that could be interpreted as giving comfort and aid to the IRA, irrespective of its inherent journalistic worth or importance. There were some brave editors and journalists who ignored these pressures and encouraged colleagues to do the same but there were many more who did not. In those days, and even now, the value and integrity of a journalist in Ireland was too often measured not by the stories he or she had published but by the stories they had ignored and by the sources they refused to talk to.

Formal, state-inspired censorship was introduced in the South in 1971 and intensified thereafter. Journalists in Ireland were and are members of the British National Union of Journalists (NUJ) and as such the local, Irish section could at any time have sought legal recourse against the restrictions. From 1973 onwards, when Ireland joined the European Union, the Irish branch could have asked NUJ headquarters in London to challenge Section 31 at the European Commission of Human Rights on their behalf or, alternatively, they could have challenged the law in the Irish courts far earlier. They chose not to. It was only in 1988, when the British government imposed formal censorship on its own broadcasters and the British section of the NUJ decided to go to Europe, that the Irish section of the union was shamed into stirring itself. Even then it was a reluctant, ponderous movement. The NUJ found it impossible to persuade any Dublin or mainstream electronic journalist to file an individual complaint, as European law required. The NUJ case was eventually taken in the name of a reporter from an Irish language radio station located in the remote fastness of the west of Ireland. More convincing evidence of how potent the combination of formal and informal censorship can be, and the willingness of journalists to co-operate in their own silencing, would be difficult to find.

THE BRITISH BROADCASTING BAN

Northern Ireland, like the South, had a long history of media control and censorship. Formal censorship was embodied in the draconian Special Powers Act of 1922, passed a year after partition was established, which gave the Unionist government the power to proscribe newspapers, books and films. Republican publications were routinely banned but the mainstream media was affected only once, when the *Derry Journal* was closed down in 1940. The electronic media was never touched by legal censorship simply because there was no need to. Until 1959 when a local commercial television station, Ulster Television, opened, public broadcasting was the exclusive preserve of the local unit of the BBC, which for the first thirty years of the state's existence, managed to completely ignore the serious divisions of Northern Ireland society and gave no coverage at all to nationalist complaints about discrimination. In the post-war years, the North's political problems began to be acknowledged but in a cautious and timorous way. Whenever the BBC crossed the line into controversy, an outcry from the Unionist government would pull it back. Between 1959 and 1968, when the civil rights movement began, government intimidation and BBC funk killed off four TV programmes.[5]

Informal, self-censorship, encouraged by often fierce public and private pressure from government, the media itself and other sections of local and British society, characterised regulation of television coverage of the post-1970 conflict both in Northern Ireland and in Britain. Between 1970 and August 1989 a total of seventy-six television programmes on Northern Ireland – documentaries, plays and even church services – were voluntarily banned, cut, postponed or refashioned because of internal and external pressure, an average of one every three months.[6] Television and radio companies, both public and private, also applied a self-imposed prohibition on interviews with paramilitary groups. The last IRA interview carried by either the BBC or ITV took place in 1974. The broadcasting companies introduced their own internal controls to regulate programmes on 'The Troubles' as early as 1971. Both the BBC and the Independent Television Authority (later the Independent Broadcasting Authority) adopted 'the reference-upwards system' that meant all items on Northern Ireland were vetted by senior management who could stop a programme from being aired or order cuts. In the BBC the permission of the Director General was needed before political figures like Gerry Adams could be interviewed, although there was no such rule for Loyalists, while internal guidelines instructed reporters to treat such interviewees in a 'forthright' and 'hostile' fashion.[7] Programmes that survived all this and which criticised British policy were often the target of fierce denunciation from government, the security apparatus and the tabloid media. Individual journalists who insisted on providing rational coverage of groups like the IRA, such as the late Mary Holland, were singled out for vilification and this served to deter others from following in her path. As in the Irish system, British and Northern journalists soon learned the career benefits that came with self-censorship. All in all, the British and Northern Ireland media were left in no doubt that if they didn't put and keep their own house in order, the government might do it for them. With scarcely a word of complaint or protest, they mostly obliged.

The British system of self-censorship arguably worked as effectively as the enforced procedure operating in the Irish Republic but carried a lower political cost. Being entirely self-imposed, it required no supervision or harsh laws, invit-

5 Moloney, E. 'Closing down the airwaves – the story of the broadcasting ban' in Rolston, B. (ed.), op. cit., 8–50 at 11.   6 Ibid.   7 Curtis, L. (1984) *Ireland: the propaganda war.* London: Pluto Press, 183.

ed no invidious comparisons with police states and was of limited propaganda value to the enemy, to groups like the Provisional IRA. How could anyone complain about, much less repudiate, a phenomenon that was invisible to all except those practising it?

It therefore came almost literally like a bolt out of the blue when on 19 October 1988, Margaret Thatcher's Home Secretary, Douglas Hurd, stood up in the House of Commons and announced that the BBC and commercial broadcasting companies had been ordered to stop carrying interviews with a range of proscribed paramilitary groups and legal political parties associated with them, notably Sinn Féin.

In one sense Thatcher's move was entirely characteristic. The Prime Minister's animosity towards current affairs television, especially the BBC, particularly over coverage of Northern Ireland affairs, was well-known and had already led to a series of very public rows between the government and broadcasters. Mrs Thatcher was also a fierce advocate of deregulating and even privatizing the electronic media, and controversial television coverage of the IRA was always a useful stick with which to beat the BBC, the principal obstacle to this ambition. The IRA's violence was also, after years of gradual decline, on an upward curve, thanks to new weapons and explosives supplied by Libya's Colonel Gaddafi, and attacks in Northern Ireland and Europe in the summer of 1988 had claimed the lives of a score or so of British security personnel, including eight soldiers killed in a landmine attack in Co. Tyrone in August 1988. The broadcasting ban was one part of a series of measures announced that autumn to curb Republicans. Nonetheless the IRA had been a much greater threat in the early 1970s and the link to Libya had been broken after the biggest shipment of all was captured when the gunrunning ship, the *Eksund*, was intercepted off the French coast. The media ban seemed largely superfluous. After all, the broadcasting media in Britain had stopped carrying interviews with the IRA fourteen years before and showed no signs of changing this stand. Nor was the electronic media exactly flooded with reportage of Sinn Féin. As Labour's Roy Hattersley pointed out during the parliamentary debate that followed Hurd's announcement, Independent Television, for example, had devoted just four minutes in the whole of 1988 to interviewing Sinn Féin or its supporters, and all but a few seconds of the coverage had been hostile.[8]

But it was the fact that the broadcasting ban applied to Sinn Féin, a legal and public party that made the measure special. Since the 1981 hunger strikes, Sinn Féin had adopted a successful strategy of standing for elections and the party's leader, Gerry Adams was by now MP for West Belfast, albeit one who declined to take his seat. This aspect of the ban highlighted the downside of Thatcher's move for the British Government. It smacked of totalitarian repression of demo-

8 Moloney, E., op. cit., 28.

cratic politics, gave the Provos ammunition to fire at the British and attracted the criticism of Britain's allies, particularly in the United States, while praise for the measure from South Africa's apartheid Prime Minister, P.W. Botha, was a huge embarrassment. There was also something of a fight back by the media. The NUJ announced it was taking the issue to Europe and there were protests, even calls for a strike. While this defiance eventually faltered, British broadcasters tried to do what their counterparts in Dublin never contemplated doing. They undermined and even ridiculed the ban by broadcasting footage of figures like Adams with actors speaking their words.

AN ACT OF REPRISAL

Apart from appearing to be another classic example of knee jerkism from Mrs Thatcher, the broadcasting ban seemed to make little sense. What was not known at this time, however, was that the Sinn Féin leadership was in secret dialogue with Mrs Thatcher's government about a plan to end the violence and agree a political settlement and that the imposition of the broadcasting ban came at a moment when the upsurge in IRA violence had derailed the talks. In this context the ban can be better understood as a punitive reprisal against Sinn Féin for this, and as such makes much more sense.

Using a Catholic priest as an intermediary, Sinn Féin president, Gerry Adams had opened contact with Thatcher's Northern Ireland Secretary, Tom King in 1986. Documents were exchanged and one outcome of all this was the production by the British side of a road map to a political settlement, one in which Sinn Féin would take its place alongside other political parties in talks about Northern Ireland's future provided the IRA ended its violence and Republicans accepted that the principle of consent would underpin any deal. It was, in many important ways, the blueprint for the later peace process.

Adams had opened the talks in great secrecy however; the IRA's leadership knew nothing about them and almost certainly would have disapproved had they known (an aspect of the dialogue that the British did not appreciate until many years later). In sharp contrast to Adams' peace diplomacy, the IRA leadership at this time was actually planning an upsurge of violence fuelled by Gaddafi's arms shipments. The capture of the last and largest Libyan shipment aboard the *Eksund* had shattered the IRA's plan but the organization decided to launch its offensive anyway, admittedly a more limited one that would deploy the weapons that had been successfully smuggled from North Africa. That campaign was launched in 1988 and although it soon ran out of steam, it reached a peak in the summer of that year. The British reaction to all this was a furious one. Gerry Adams, through his clerical intermediary, was preaching peace but the IRA was killing with greater gusto than before. Adams was making fools of the British, or so they thought. With Thatcher's approval, Tom King, whose Somerset home was put under IRA surveillance during this upsurge and whose anger against the Sinn Féin leader had a personal edge, called off the talks and later that year Adams and his colleagues were forced off the airwaves. Seen against this background, the 1988 broadcasting ban was not so much an effort to control media coverage of 'The Troubles' as it was an act of retribution against the republican political leadership for its perceived sleight of hand.[9] But as we all know, the infant peace process survived. Just six years later the IRA called its first ceasefire and by 1998 the road map generated by Tom King and Gerry Adams was an actuality.

CENSORSHIP, 'THE TROUBLES' AND THE PEACE PROCESS

The success of the peace process therefore prompts two questions about the role played by media censorship. What impact did media censorship in general have on 'The Troubles'? And, in particular, did the 1988 broadcasting ban help or hinder the peace process? Censorship was always justified on the grounds, to use Margaret Thatcher's words, that it would deny terrorists the oxygen of publicity and thereby hasten their demise. The proof of that pudding is in the eating. The IRA's campaign lasted one year short of a quarter of a century, the lengthiest period of political violence in Irish history, and it lasted so long largely because the IRA had no difficulty recruiting people who were prepared to go out and kill, be killed or risk imprisonment, sometimes for lengthy periods, in its name. Those people were motivated not by radio or TV programmes but by personal experience, such as violence at the hands of the security forces, or by wrongs visited on their community by the security forces or the British Government. No amount of censorship would have changed that. Far from shortening 'The Troubles' or reducing support for the IRA, there is as strong an argument that censorship actually made the conflict more long lasting and created support for the IRA. It did so in two ways. Firstly censorship made it much more difficult to explain why it was that people joined the IRA and killed in its name. As a result public debate about the IRA was not only severely limited but also often misinformed. And if public opinion was ill-informed or misinformed about the organization and its motivation what did that say about policy decisions affecting the IRA made by government? The second way censorship worsened matters was that it discouraged or delayed the media from examining issues, such as miscarriages of justice, whose earlier resolution would have restored or boosted confidence in political

9 Moloney, E. (2002) *A secret history of the IRA*. London: Allen Lane, chapter eight.

methods. The fact that for years journalists refused to cover stories like the Birmingham Six or Guildford Four out of fear that they would be tainted as IRA supporters, surely strengthened the view in areas like west Belfast that only violence could change things, that going through the system was a waste of time. Censorship helped to nurture the grievances that fuelled 'The Troubles'.

The issue of the 1988 broadcasting ban may be different though. The ban intensified Sinn Féin's isolation just at a point when the party's leadership was anxious to leave violence behind and to join conventional politics. The ban was the high point of a campaign to quarantine the party. Already senior Catholic clerics had refused to meet elected Sinn Féin representatives like Adams, as had government ministers on both sides of the border, while community bodies with even tenuous links to the Provos were denied government funding or assistance. Imposing the broadcasting ban on top of all this and adding it to Section 31 in the Republic, meant that it was now official policy throughout Ireland and Britain to treat Sinn Féin as pariahs until such time as the IRA ended its violence.

Whether, or by how much, this accelerated Sinn Féin's movement towards the peace process are necessarily matters of conjecture. But it was clear to many of those whose job it was to observe and report on the Provisional leadership during this time that their exclusion from society deeply rankled, that they yearned to be treated with the same respect as conventional elected politicians were. And it was perhaps no coincidence that when the peace process began to get really serious, in 1993 and 1994, the removal of media censorship became a bargaining chip in the negotiating process, first as an incentive offered by the government in Dublin to call an IRA ceasefire, and then as a reward from the British after the ceasefire was declared. The answer to the questions about the impact of censorship is therefore mixed. It both made 'The Troubles' worse and last longer and it also helped to bring them to an end. But the differing effects were due, not to any impact on the media or the media's impact on the IRA, but to the political evolution and transition of the republican leadership over a long period of time.

Formal censorship of the media had ended by 1995 but its informal manifestation lived on. By this stage, self-censorship had existed for nearly twenty-five years; it had become an organic and institutionalized part of Irish journalism and could not be removed by the stroke of a ministerial pen, as Section 31 and the broadcasting ban had been. The practice of not delving too deeply into controversial stories, of asking first what the political and career downside was before pursuing a story or an angle on a story was by now as instinctive to journalists in Ireland as riding a bicycle. But now it was the turn of the peace process rather than the war process to profit from it.

Before, when the IRA's war was raging, a journalist would worry about being regarded as a fellow-traveller for writing or wanting to broadcast a story that, for instance, critiques government policy. Now they worried about being regarded by officialdom as being 'unhelpful to the peace process', as the phrase had it, for asking hard questions about its genesis and direction, questions the Sinn Féin leadership would rather weren't asked. In the past, Republicans, the IRA and Sinn Féin were the principal victims of censorship; now they became its main beneficiary. The journey from war into peace involved, from the republican viewpoint, enormous ideological flip-flops. These included, to name but one example, accepting the idea that unionist consent was a precondition for Irish unity and independence, and that amounted to a rejection of one of the foundation stones of republican philosophy. The peace process meant Republicans accepting institutions they had died and killed for to overthrow, from the local parliament at Stormont to the policing and criminal justice system. It meant embracing a system they had once angrily proclaimed was rotten with corruption and beyond reform.

The journey undertaken by the Provisional leadership was a huge one – perhaps the most significant and far-reaching in the history of Ireland's search for independence, yet it is also one of the least investigated and most un-probed stories of all time. Journalists all too often resisted digging into the causes of the peace process and did so as assiduously as they had avoided examining the causes of the conflict – and for the same reason: the fear of what they would find. And in the case of those who were tempted to delve and excavate, there were always those hardworking, vigilant Sinn Féin officials around to remind them of the consequences if they did, whether it be to punish them by cutting off access to the party and its leaders or to whisper behind hands to all that would listen that this or that reporter was far too close to dissidents. In the salad days of Section 31, Workers' Party apparatchiks in RTÉ and elsewhere had enforced censorship with relish; twenty years later their erstwhile comrades undertook the same task with the same enthusiasm and using methods that were remarkably similar.

Inevitably, one question demands an answer. Could the process and the republican leadership have survived rigorous scrutiny by the media? We'll probably never know the answer but at the very least, it is arguable that if they could not have survived, then the peace process itself was fundamentally flawed and doomed. On the other hand, if the foundations of the process were as strong and healthy as its architects claimed, then they would have withstood the closest examination. In the meantime, censorship, now voluntarily imposed by the media itself rather than by government, lives on in Ireland. And so do the methods by which it is enforced: fear and intimidation.

Part III

Media, censorship and the public sphere

8 / Calling the tune: the media, the state and the public's right to know

HELEN SHAW

All governments seek to control information, even in the healthiest democracies. It is the tension between a public's right to know and the state's desire to manage information that creates particular friction between the media and government. That tension is heightened during war or civil conflict and most sharply felt between the public media and the state. Former Director General of the BBC, Greg Dyke, who was forced to resign over the Hutton Report, said during the Iraq war in 2003 that there had to be a 'healthy tension' between the BBC and the British government as the BBC's duty was to inform the public while the government needed to win a war.[1] And information, as we saw during the Hutton Inquiry into the events surrounding the death of Dr David Kelly, a British weapons expert on Iraq, became not just a tool of that war but also a means of prosecuting it.

The Hutton Inquiry highlighted the complex interface between the public-funded broadcaster and the state with the Gilligan/Campbell media row been seen as the worst breakdown in relations for decades.[2] At the heart of that breakdown were not just careless journalism, over-sized egos and a tragic suicide, but ultimately whether the government manipulated the facts to make the case for war. For the BBC it became a trial on the role of public broadcasting itself.

WHOSE SIDE ARE YOU ON?

The Blair government's perception that the BBC was not 'behind' the war coloured everything and it underscores the difficult interface between a public-funded broadcaster and the state. Public media's credibility and reputation is

1 Greg Dyke addressing Harvard School of Business, Harvard University, April 2003.   2 Alastair Campbell, head of Downing Street's Communications, became obsessed with Andrew Gilligan's coverage of the Iraq war for the BBC's flagship *Today* programme, describing it as biased and anti-government. Campbell's repeated pressure on the BBC's News Division during the war is seen as one of the factors in the BBC's over-defence of Gilligan's shaky reportage of David Kelly's views following Gilligan's fateful early morning two-way report with the *Today* programme, 29 May 2003, which sparked the events leading to the Hutton Inquiry. Lord Hutton's report was published on 28 January 2004, and severely criticized the BBC and its editorial structures while accepting the government, and indeed Campbell's, version of events. See John Cassidy, 'The Kelly affair', *New Yorker*, January 2004 and the Hutton Report on the BBC website www.bbc.co.uk.

based on independence yet the state often sees it as part of its apparatus – particularly when that state is under attack. The Falklands War in 1982, which saw the British prosecute a war with Argentina over the Falklands islands, was one of the last major flashpoints between broadcaster and government. Then the BBC came under significant pressure from Mrs Thatcher's government to be more pro-British in its war coverage. The government objected to the BBC maintaining balance during the war and using, in its news reports, the phrase the 'British government' and 'British troops' rather than 'we' and 'ours'. It was a confrontation that the then BBC Director General, Alasdair Milne, won and which allowed the BBC to maintain that position during the Iraq war.

Take the desire of a government to control information at the time of war, into civil conflict or terrorist situations and the pressure to shape the news becomes stronger. George Bush's post 9/11 mantra, 'you're either with us, or against us', had a profound impact on the news media in the US. Andrew Heyward, President of CBS News, took the opposite view to Greg Dyke when he told an audience at Harvard University that he was 'rooting for the US to win' in any conflict and that 'there is little place for objectivity when your country is at war.'[3]

CREATING A CLIMATE OF CENSORSHIP

Terrorism, the direct targeting of civilians and non-combatants, creates an environment where the media, whether through commercial pressure if they are conglomerates, or state influence if they are public, are frequently pushed to censor views. The unsavoury becomes unpalatable and it is easier to exclude rather than include. In Ireland, the escalation of civil violence in Northern Ireland through the early seventies and the impact of the 1974 Dublin and Monaghan bombings, which killed thirty-three civilians, created a political and indeed public culture that allowed state censorship to thrive. Section 31 of the Broadcasting Act from 1971 to 1994 forced RTÉ, then the only Irish source of national broadcast news, to expunge the voices and opinions of not just the outlawed, armed, paramilitary groups but also their political wings, like Sinn Féin. Those who were banned and the groups to which they belonged, became the demonised creatures of the conflict and several observers, including author and journalist Ed Moloney, maintain that the prolonged enforcement of a Section 31 media culture delayed the peace settlement and cost lives.[4]

3 Andrew Heyward, addressing a public audience at the J.F. Kennedy School of Government, Harvard, October 2002.   4 Haughey, N. 'Censorship may have cost lives, says editor' in *Irish Times*, 21 February 2000 (coverage of Ed Moloney's speech at an Irish Council for Civil Liberties. See also this volume.)

The US media experience post-9/11, as TV anchor Dan Rather put it in May 2002, allowed a climate of patriotism and fear to foster self-censorship. As one senior editor said, the fear of being labelled unpatriotic was and is enough to make many journalists stop asking questions.[5] In an era of new McCarthyism the worst label you can carry in the United States now is not 'communist' but 'unpatriotic' and 'anti-American'. As was the case in Ireland during the years when Section 31 was in place, the rewards for challenging the consensus has been to be pushed to the margins of political debate, a fate that befell the late Edward Said.

The difference in the US is that media control of information is largely commercially based – it is not good corporate business to be seen as anything less than flag-waving – while in Ireland, and in Britain, the state's desire to control the political situation and public information lead to legislative controls on broadcasters. While forms of self-censorship controls already operated, the British government only introduced a broadcasting ban on proscribed organisations and their political wings in October 1988.[6]

In Ireland the broadcasting ban altered the information Irish audiences could receive and profoundly changed the nature of broadcasting, public debate, and journalism for that generation, as other contributors to this volume attest. For the public, and indeed many journalists, censorship, like blinkers on a horse, created its own limited vision so that the censored world soon became the accepted reality. The absent voices allowed citizens in the Republic to distance themselves from the North and view the rolling violence as evidence that 'they' were mad or evil. In the early 1990s human rights activists based in Dublin could talk fluently of solutions for South Africa, Palestine or Ethiopia but dismiss Northern Ireland as 'intractable'. In the Republic, the broadcasting ban operated in a period of heightened political polarisation, conditioned by the growing violence of the 1970s and the Maze hunger strike in 1981, which further pushed people into entrenched positions. Those who opposed the ban were labelled 'fellow travellers', apologists for terrorism or 'hush puppies', the label that commentator, Eoghan Harris, used to tar journalists/producers who opposed Section 31. Such labels implied that those opposed to censorship were little more than provisional IRA mouthpieces. Not surprising the majority of journalists, who were not politically motivated, and nowhere near Belfast or Derry, kept their heads down. Once mud was thrown it was hard to shake off.

I arrived in RTÉ's Radio Centre in 1988 as a young radio producer straight from the Belfast bureau of the *Irish Times* where I had been based for some years. I was used to the cut and thrust of Northern Irish 'politics' and had covered the

5 Jodie Allen, US News and Report, speaking to a lunch meeting at Harvard University, October 2002. 6 Moloney, E. 'Closing Down the Airwaves – the Story of the Broadcasting Ban' in Rolston. B. (ed) (1991) *The media and Northern Ireland: covering the Troubles*. London: Macmillan. See also Ed Moloney, this volume, above.

spectrum from the post Anglo-Irish Agreement riots to the emerging peace process. I had been the beat reporter on the 1987 UK General Election that saw Gerry Adams elected in west Belfast, and arrived on the scene of the Enniskillen bombing, when the IRA killed eleven civilians, just shortly after the explosion. I had become used to reporting news that often people did not want to hear. As a print journalist I was convinced the broadcasting ban was counter-productive but even within quality newspapers the debate over what could be said or written raged. The *Irish Times* Belfast office enjoyed an often tense dialogue with the Dublin head office and just before I arrived, as a very young reporter, editorial differences had led to the departure of the then Northern Editor, Ed Moloney, and one of the most skilled writers on the scene, Fionnuala O'Connor. Writing about Northern Ireland was not a 'safe' correspondence.

In RTÉ I hoped to bring my print experience to radio. I recognised the difficulties of working with Section 31 but felt it was important for journalists like me, with some understanding of northern politics, to try to tell that story on a national basis. I was, and am, politically unaffiliated and have always worked by the rule that a journalist has no business joining anything except a trade union. That summer of 1988, setting up a Belfast programme on the first season of the *Pat Kenny Show* I asked a researcher to check some facts and run it past the political parties, including Sinn Féin. She looked at me with some horror and said, 'But we're not allowed do that.' I had to remind her that the law prevented us from recording and broadcasting an interview with a member of a proscribed organisation but we could still pick up the phone and do our job. Section 31 had created an environment where people avoided the 'banned' groups, avoided the potential for contamination, and left it to a handful of security correspondents to do the dark and shady, top-secret, 'I've just been talking to a man in a balaclava' routine.

SELF-CENSORSHIP

In many ways the Section 31 period, and indeed the lack of campaign against it within the Irish broadcast industry showed that self-censorship was as powerful as state censorship. In an environment where the public broadcaster had been clearly sanctioned through state actions such as the dismissal of the RTÉ Authority in 1972, and the sentencing of Kevin O'Kelly for failing to reveal his sources, it is hardly surprising that the subsequent RTÉ response was not only to enforce the law but to interpret it quite strictly.[7] Like other colleagues, I recall being pulled aside because someone, talking about gardening to Marian Finucane on *Liveline*, turned out to be a member of Sinn Féin, and how reports on trade union

7 See the chapter by Desmond Fisher, above, for a description of this case.

disputes were dropped because the official turned out to be a member of Sinn Féin. That official, Larry O'Toole, later won a Supreme Court challenge to Section 31 in 1992 over RTÉ's decision not to broadcast an interview with him during the Gateaux strike.[8]

Journalists and producers were forced to police the airwaves and once someone had a northern accent and/or came from a nationalist/loyalist community one had to ask the 'Are you or have you ever been … ?' question and if in doubt run the name past the Belfast office in case RTÉ was embarrassed by someone going to the newspapers saying we had breached Section 31. The amount of energy that went into policing the ban meant many programme makers avoided Northern Ireland because it was trouble and time consuming. Everything had to be recorded, edited and scrutinised and ways of achieving balance found within the law. Live programmes became hazardous and one had to argue the case to make them. Lists of 'safe' people who could 'represent' the viewpoint of the banned groups or communities were continually sought and many Belfast based journalists made healthy side earnings by being the 'interpreter' between the banned and the broadcaster.

Equally, many programme-makers after a lifetime working under Section 31 – and with a personal distance from Northern Ireland – simply did not want to do those programmes, or to encourage them being made, because the going wisdom was 'It's boring.' Things you do not understand which go on repetitively, without a support context, are boring. That switch-off remains part of the long-term legacy of censorship and making audiences engage in the story today is part of the challenge facing journalists reporting Northern Ireland.

Many of us made programmes as best we could and walked that thin line between journalistic integrity and complicity. Lots of programmes were not made, many people were never interviewed and the historical archive of RTÉ, let alone the contemporary understanding of events, is all the poorer as a result. Try to make a documentary on any part of the history of Northern Ireland and the blanks are more telling than what remains. In hindsight, it is necessary to acknowledge that the issues were always highly nuanced and not as often portrayed, black and white, full of innocence or guilt, action or shame. But equally we have to recognize the highly politicised nature of all broadcasting work at that period, even up until 1998 and the Good Friday Agreement, and see the need to explore the long term consequences of that regime of censorship, silence and caution. The period demonstrates the need to create firewalls between the state and public media to ensure independence, to protect the public's right to know on the grounds that a functioning democracy needs all voices, even those speaking against democracy itself, exposed to public scrutiny.

8 Cleary, C. 'A trade unionist who took RTÉ to court' in *Irish Times*, 18 May 1998.

OPPOSING SECTION 31

The RTÉ NUJ Branch meetings on the subject (in those days post the Jenny McGeever incident)[9] were volatile and politicised making it difficult for anyone whose opposition to Section 31 was journalistic rather than politically based. It made it extremely difficult for many young journalists who simply wanted to tell the story, warts and all. Senior news journalists with big reputations and indeed status were powerful forces to counter and much of the debate on the conse-quences of Section 31 took place in an emotional and subjective arena. It is a mat-ter of public record (and is dealt with elsewhere in this volume)[10] that the then Workers' Party held significant influence in parts of the news media, in both RTÉ and newspapers. That, combined with centrist Fine Gael/Labour/Fianna Fáil support for the ban, meant that the voices raising questions were margin-alised and dismissed. As a print reporter I was accused of 'going native' when I made my views on the ban clear in discussions in Belfast. Later as a radio pro-ducer, like others, I was often reminded that I was on a short-term contract and vulnerable when I became involved in the broader NUJ/SIPTU campaign against Section 31.

On the other hand, for those whose opposition was political, whose views were predicated on a sympathy or support for the republican movement, the world was equally monotone. As an RTÉ NUJ representative, at an AGM in Glasgow in 1989, I opposed a motion linking the NUJ to a United Ireland/British withdrawal stance and was accused of being a 'west-Brit'. For me the two, opposition to Section 31 and to the NUJ taking a political position on Northern Ireland were the same – journalism was and is about telling all sides of the story – not taking a side.

Within BBC London, because of the sheer benefit of distance and location, the atmosphere was different. In the United Kingdom, broadcasting censorship was in place for a shorter period and had a less profound impact. Broadcasters soon came up with the bizarre voice-over solution that gave unemployed actors in Belfast work as the public persona for the 'banned' – and some of the actors did more with the scripts than the gagged politicians, like Gerry Adams and Mar-tin McGuinness, could ever have achieved. Indeed, the British ban and the sub-sequent international media attention increased the profile of people like Adams in the US and across continental Europe.

But in BBC Northern Ireland, a more intimate environment than London, sim-ilar tensions and emotions to those that dominated in RTÉ prevailed. Even by

9 For an account of the Jenny McGeever case, read Horgan, J. 'Journalists and censorship: a case history of the NUJ in Ireland and the broadcasting ban, 1971–1994'. *Journalism Studies*, 3 (3) 2002, 377–92. 10 See the chapter by Colum Kenny, above.

1996 when I joined BBC NI as a news editor the public sensitivities to hearing or seeing the once 'banned' were real. The IRA Canary Wharf bomb in February 1996 broke the 1994 ceasefire that had prompted the lifting of the broadcasting bans and consequently local broadcasters, like the BBC, were under significant pressure to re-introduce self-censorship. John Cushnahan, former Alliance leader, and then a Fine Gael MEP, went as far as to call for a re-introduction of the broadcasting ban to get the 'apologists', as he termed them, off the air.

NEWS MANAGEMENT IN THE WIDER ARENA

Both RTÉ and BBC NI shared an emotional and human proximity to the story – and indeed violence – that coloured how people perceived the situation. For both societies the counter-balance of BBC and ITV from London ensured a wider debate. The growing presence, by the 1990s of global news broadcasters, like CNN or Sky, equally made a return to the strict Section 31 framework unlikely in that the majority of TV viewers in Ireland now had access to a multitude of news options from different media platforms, including satellite and the internet. Ten years after the lifting of Section 31 (though the legislation was only finally repealed in 2001), it is time not just to re-assess what happened in Ireland but to examine the lessons we can provide to other societies attempting to grapple with the issue of civil violence, terrorism and censorship.

Among the first actions of President Vladimir Putin's administration following the Moscow siege, in October 2002, was a media clampdown with a proposal to censor media coverage of 'terrorism'. Following considerable international criticism, Putin eventually vetoed the law, although media self-censorship largely fulfilled the promise of the vetoed bill. The only independent national TV station was closed down in June 2003. By September 2003 a media law restricting political commentary and coverage was introduced prompting some newspapers to say it was now impossible to cover politics in Russia. The new law allows for any media outlet to be shut down during the electoral process after two warnings.[11]

In Spain the government of Jose Maria Aznar equally took the opportunity of the US declared 'war on terrorism' to curtail civil rights. In March 2003 a daily newspaper, the Basque language *Egunkaria*, was closed down by the state on the basis of an alleged link to ETA – the violent Basque separatist group – despite a lack of evidence and the fact that the newspaper was funded by the regional government run by moderate anti-ETA Basques.[12] Many commentators saw it as political opportunism to silence a regional voice, in the run-up to elections, under

11 Walsh, N. 'Putin puts Soviet bar on poll coverage' in *The Guardian*, 9 September 2003.　12 Tremlett, G. 'Fourth estate – or fifth column?' in *The Guardian*, 3 March 2003.

the all-embracing banner of 'anti-terrorism'. For constitutional Basques, however, an attack on Basque media was seen as an echo of Franco's policies and rather than diminish support for the separatist movement the closure of *Egunkaria*, the arrest of its editor and the alleged torture of the editor in custody, provided the grounds to justify it.

The broadcasting bans operated, in theory, to starve the paramilitaries of 'the oxygen of publicity' yet what they achieved was to drive those communities further out of the mainstream and break any links of communication between the mainstream and the subversives. The view of one time British Secretary of State for Northern Ireland, Roy Mason, in 1976 was that all coverage, even of acts of violence, should be denied media attention, by compulsory order if required, on the basis that the paramilitaries would fade away. Mason's belief, that one had to tackle the knowledge of what existed rather than what existed, is at the heart of the case for censorship. Certainly all sides were engaged in a publicity battle but the idea that without media coverage the violence would have ended or that the media is something to be switched on and off shows how government, whether conservative or labour, views the need to control and indeed manipulate what the public does or does not know.

In South Africa despite decades of media censorship and state TV portraying a white Afrikaner view of the world, violence and indeed support for the ANC grew. In 1994, in the days running up to the first multi-racial elections, I saw, as an international observer in a farming town in the Karoo, the visible transformation of South African television as the colour and language, literally, of the news anchors changed. The censored TV world had not stopped the ANC but what it had done was allowed many ordinary white people to live in denial, believing the blinkered reality presented by the teatime news.

Media censorship did not undermine republican community support for the IRA in Northern Ireland, although it may have affected the electoral performance of Sinn Féin given the loss of Gerry Adams' west Belfast seat in 1992 during the period of the British broadcasting ban. It did however make it more difficult for the Dublin based media and political establishment to accept when John Hume, in 1988, started meeting and talking to the very people who were deemed too terrible to broadcast. Section 31, which had the effect of demonizing many of the players in the northern conflict, increased the isolation of audiences in the Republic from the Northern Irish story so that the story could be readily dismissed and switched off. A small society seeing violence against shoppers, unarmed fathers switching on the engine of their car and being blown apart in front of their families or builders working for the 'wrong' side shot dead, will naturally find it easier to exclude the voices associated with such horror. Journalists are citizens and human beings too and for many the simple response was once censorship became law it had to be respected and observed.

THE EROSION OF THE PUBLIC SPHERE

Censorship is always a complex and multi-layered experience. At a European Broadcasting Union conference for Radio in Turkey not long after 9/11, in April 2002, I shared a platform, representing RTÉ as Director of Radio, with my Spanish colleagues on the issue of media, censorship and conflict. In an audience that included many countries and communities torn apart by civil violence, including Algeria and the former Yugoslavia states, let alone Turkey itself, this was a sensitive subject. I told the story of Ireland and Section 31 and said that the impact and damage of twenty-three years of censorship had still to be assessed but that it clearly had had a profound impact on the development of broadcast journalism and on the public's understanding of the conflict itself. For my Spanish colleagues still caught in the midst of ETA violence, where journalists have themselves been targeted, the issue was one where those who denied democratic means should be denied democratic rights. It is often understandably hard to see beyond that when your own colleagues have been killed and maimed and your own society is under attack.

We must protect democratic society against the use of the media as propaganda, as the Nazis employed it in the 1930s or the way radio was used in the fermenting of genocide in Rwanda in 1994, but ultimately we need to protect the ideal of the media, particularly the public media, as a forum for debate and communication to secure the basis of our own civil society. And that may mean giving access to those voices that speak against our society and our democracy. In the US, post-9/11, a culture of media censorship was created, not by law, but by fear and by the government's repetition of key concepts, such as a direct connection between Saddam Hussein and 9/11, despite the lack of evidence to support it. I spent a year there, based at Harvard University, from the first anniversary of 9/11 to the second and found the climate of unquestioning patriotism, particularly on TV news, reminiscent of the blinkered mentality created during the Irish ban. The emotional trauma of 9/11 on the US psyche, and the stance taken by the Bush administration, hit a pause button on the critical faculties of the news media.

From October 2002 and into 2003, an average of 60–70 per cent of Americans stated in opinion polls that Saddam Hussein was directly linked to the attacks.[13] Yet the fact that the public believed something that was false, and which President Bush one year later admitted was baseless, showed how little challenge

13 Zeller, T. 'How Americans link Iraq and Sept. 11' in *New York Times* (survey of polls), 1 March 2003.

or debate was taking place in the media. The US Iraq war coverage, when put in counter-position with the BBC coverage, showed a media reluctant to ask questions and prepared to take Pentagon releases as their single source. The subsequent Hutton Inquiry in the UK forced the US media to explore the manipulation of information in the run-up to the war in Bush's State of the Union speech and Colin Powell's presentations to the UN.

Violence, particularly against civilians, creates an environment where human rights, including the concept of the right to express an opinion, as enshrined in Article 19 of the UN Charter on Human Rights, can be seen as a luxury and something to be suspended when under attack.[14] The difficulty is that without a functioning news media, seeking to air and debate conflict rather than suppress it, the culture of violence goes underground and thrives rather than dies. In the end, if the objective is to reduce violence and conflict, there is no evidence that political censorship works. In fact it can give mystique to the unheard and enhance that community's sense of oppression and exclusion. At the same time it makes the concept of a negotiated settlement more difficult to achieve and to sell.

Ireland's experience of broadcast censorship should become an international case study in the consequences of excluding and silencing voices in situations of civil conflict so that other democracies may learn from our experience rather than allowing fear, hysteria or misguided patriotism dictate the limits of a free and democratic media. Freedom of speech and opinion – freedom to debate, to report, to know – these are not freedoms to be parked when society is under attack. That is the time when we need them most.

---

14 The UN Charter on Human Rights, Article 19, states that 'everyone has the right to freedom of opinion and expression; this right includes freedom to hold opinions without interference and to seek, receive and impart information and ideas through any media and regardless of frontiers'.

9 / A deceived audience or a discerning audience? News management and the threat to the public sphere

MARY P. CORCORAN

'The benefits of a restriction such as Section 31 are questionable as must be the case wherever the public is closed off from political information that concerns it'.[1]

THE IDEA OF THE PUBLIC SPHERE

One of the basic principles of democracy is the ideal of the public sphere, that notional space wherein the public formulate, debate and exchange opinion. Public opinion ideally is conceived as the outcome of the cut and thrust of debate that occurs in the public sphere. At the dawn of the twenty-first century, there is a fairly widespread view that while the public sphere as a democratic domain may be more necessary than ever, it is increasingly difficult to locate. A recent essay in the *Economist* contends that the modern equivalent of the coffee house, wherein the seeds of the democratic project were sown in the seventeenth and eighteenth centuries, may be the internet. The internet is no longer solely the province of military intelligence and computer boffins, but has grown to become 'a nexus of commercial, journalistic and political interchange'.[2] Nevertheless, it must also be acknowledged that the internet is not a universally accessible medium, and that many of the uses to which it is put do not fall within the rather high-minded aspirations of those who would see it as a new digital public sphere.

The rise of infotainment programming and the concomitant dumbing down of culture; the expansion in the number and range of media platforms; and the proliferation of news managers and news management techniques have combined to fracture the notion of a body politic, alienating us from the public sphere. Conglomeration, commercialisation and commodification characterize the media landscape today. In these circumstances, public service broadcasting is often held up as the last refuge of the public sphere, a far cry from Habermas' eighteenth-century coffee house, but an enduring forum nevertheless, for promoting reasoned argument and disputation. It is to the public service broadcasters that we repair when seeking balance, objectivity and impartiality in the reporting of the

---

1 *Irish Times* editorial, 'A blunt instrument', 11 June 1991.   2 'The internet in a cup', *The Economist*, 20 December 2003.

issues of the day. But even public service broadcasting is not immune to the machinations of its political masters. Witness the unrelenting pressure to which the BBC was subjected by Downing Street in 2003 over its coverage of the war in Iraq. Politicians, and the spin masters working on their behalf, to a greater or lesser extent, seek to control access, to shape 'their message' and to determine where and how that message is diffused. Though its independence is a sacred pillar of the western democratic tradition, public service broadcasting can be made to bend to the will of its political masters. When this happens broadcasting loses something of its reputation for independence, journalists baulk at covering 'difficult' and 'dangerous' stories, a chill wind blows through the newsroom and the audience inevitably is short-changed.

This is what happened in Ireland, when in 1971, restrictions were imposed on RTÉ, the public broadcaster, preventing the station from broadcasting interviews with members of proscribed organizations. The provisions of Section 31 were later eloquently justified by the Minister for Posts and Telegraphs, Conor Cruise O'Brien. In particular, he argued that, 'the democratic state has the right to enact repressive legislation, provided that it represses the right things in the right way, and by means that are adequate but not excessive'.[3] Leaving aside the question of whether it is ever possible to enact repressive legislation that is not inherently open to abuse or prone to create unintended effects, let us consider one of the key presuppositions that underlies all legislation of this nature. Restrictions on the scope of political broadcasting are enacted in the interest of democracy, and logically, therefore, they must be in the public interest. It is for the good of the public that the public service broadcasters must be inveigled to restrict their coverage and suspend their commitment to balanced reporting. Clearly, from the point of view of the legislators, neither journalists nor the audiences they serve can be trusted to handle difficult and complex political positions.

In this chapter I want to critically examine this thesis by focusing on three constituencies: the political class that enacts legislation including legislation that regulates the mass media, the journalists who gather, process and disseminate the news and finally the news audience itself. I will argue that a particular conceptualisation of journalists and the media audience they serve underlies attempts by governments to restrict access and coverage in the mass media. Furthermore, journalists and editors at the coalface of news production, work with a particular conceptualisation of their audience in mind. Finally, we will speculate as to whether or not the audience is capable of exercising a critical reading when confronted with broadcasting output that has been put through the censorship wringer.

---

3 See the chapter by Conor Cruise O'Brien, above.

THEORIES OF THE MASS MEDIA AUDIENCE

The decision to impose censorship through whatever means, is based on the rather antiquated view that the media produce information as 'magic bullets' that have a direct and persuasive effect on those who are exposed to them. After all, the 'oxygen of publicity' afforded to deviant or socially sanctioned groups would be harmless if it simply evaporated into thin air. The view of the media audience as susceptible to media messages harks back to the rather pessimistic prognosis put forward by Walter Lippman in his seminal book, *Public Opinion*.[4] Lippman saw the newly emerged media audience at the dawn of the twentieth century as an undifferentiated and minimally educated mass that would be easily manipulated by the new 'psuedo-environment' that had inserted itself between it – the public – and social reality. The view that the mediation of reality through film, radio, newspapers and comics is deleterious to the health of the body politic, held sway up until the Second World War, chiefly because of the concerns that industrialisation had indeed created a mass society of anomic and disconnected individuals and also, because of the visible rise of Fascism and its reliance on propaganda techniques during the 1930s.[5] With the introduction of more sophisticated scientific tools for assessing the values, beliefs and orientations of the public from the 1950s, an alternative view of the mass audience emerged. Reflecting the general shift toward functionalist analysis in sociology generally, media analysts argued that the appropriate question is not what does the mass media do to the audience, but rather what does the audience do with the mass media. Researchers set out to answer this question empirically, focusing on the uses that people make of the mass media, and the gratifications that they derive from such usage. Studies such as the classic, *The People's Choice*, used panel survey techniques to test public opinion both before and after exposure to media in the context of an election campaign.[6] The findings supported the minimal effects thesis, that is, the media were found to play a crucial role in reinforcing existing beliefs. Its conversion effect – its capacity to change pre-existing political positions – was found to be minimal. Audiences are, generally speaking, drawn to information that confirms rather than challenges their pre-existing beliefs.

Audience research fell somewhat out of favour during the 1960s and 1970s when media studies turned away from the empirical tradition and toward more theoretically rigorous examinations of the political economy of mass communication, and the ideological presuppositions embedded in media structures, processes and content. Marxist sociologists tended to see television primarily as an agent of domination within societies organised along capitalist principles. Recalling the

4 Lippman, W. (1922) *Public opinion.* New York: Macmillan.   5 Gurevitch, M. et al. (eds) (1982) *Culture, society and the media.* London: Matheus.   6 Lazarsfeld, P. et al. (1948) *The people's choice: how the voter makes up his mind in a presidential campaign.* Columbia: Columbia University Press.

pessimistic analysis of the impact of popular culture put forward by the Frankfurt School in the 1930s, analysts argued that television presents a distorted picture of reality to a largely passive audience thereby inculcating an unquestioning allegiance to a bourgeois value system. Thus, television and other media platforms, help to shore up the status quo. George Gerbner pioneered cultivation analysis in the United States, arguing that through the act of watching television, people are effectively persuaded to accept a view of society, and of their place in it, that confirms and reinforces their subordination.[7] In particular, Gerbner argues that television viewing of violence has the effect of domesticating its audience, making us fearful of the social world outside our hall doors and more submissive to authority.

A contrary perspective on the relationship between television messages and the audience is generally referred to in the literature as the dominant audience view.[8] This tends to see the media text not as monolithic, with a single preferred meaning, but rather as containing a number of possible meanings, and therefore, allowing a range of audience interpretations. Furthermore, this perspective allows us to view the audience as active and not passive. Audience members are engaged by the media text to the extent that they analyse and critically assess it. In other words, the audience is free to make what it will of the messages it receives. Even if the audience believes a dominant message that is reiterated in the media, that does not mean that that belief will be activated in the formulation of opinion on related issues. Audiences can and do demonstrate considerable resilience in terms of their resistance to 'media' viewpoints that contradict their own worldview. Likewise, audiences are capable of compartmentalising views that often appear contradictory. We shall return to this point below when we examine Irish audiences.

That (erroneous) construction of the audience as highly malleable has changed little over time, and has formed the basis for first, cultural and later political censorship on the island of Ireland (see other contributions in this volume). But it is not just a distrust of the audience that the government betrays, it is also a distrust of journalists – those who are responsible for selecting, framing and packaging the news for the viewing and listening audience. Since the foundation of the state, successive Irish Governments have betrayed a lack of trust in the capacity of Irish broadcast journalists to carry out their jobs with objectivity and impartiality.

7 See for example, Gerbner, G. 'Violence in television drama: trends and symbolic functions' in Comstock, G.A. & Rubinstein, E.A. (eds) (1972) *Television and social behavior*, vol. 1: *Content and control*. Washington, D.C.: US Government Printing Office; Gebner, G. & Gross, L. 'Living with television: the violence profile' in *Journal of Communications* (26) 1976, 172–99; Gerbner, G. et al. (1979) 'Television viewing and fear of victimization: specification or spuriousness'. Annenberg School of Communications, University of Pennsylvania.   8 Abercrombie, N. (1996) *Television and Society*. Cambridge: Polity Press.

There is always a fear that if the journalist is not with us then he or she must be against us. Hence, at least part of the rationale underlying political censorship is the belief that journalists will use their media platforms to support their own radical or subversive agendas. It is to a discussion of this view that we now turn.

IRISH JOURNALISTS AND THEIR VIEW OF
THE AUDIENCES THEY SERVE

Several years ago, writing in his capacity as editor of the *Sunday Tribune*, Vincent Browne argued that 'the media is not reflective of the full range of views and opinions in Irish society . . . journalists and editors in the main hold views that are representative of a small minority of opinion. Journalists are in the main, very much more liberal in their outlook than is true generally.'[9] This is a view that has been advanced within academic discourse in the United States[10] and voiced many times in public discourse. The political persuasions of journalists are usually determined by self-assessment on left-right scales, by questions on party preference and questions about their views on specific issues.[11] A survey carried out among Irish daily news journalists in Ireland at the end of the 1990s gives us some insight into the political orientations of Irish journalists. This survey was conducted as part of a larger Media and Democracy project directed by Professor Tom Patterson of Harvard University.[12] Patterson and Donsbach have analysed their data on political partisanship for the five participating countries in the Media and Democracy study,[13] so it is possible to make some comparisons between their findings and the responses obtained from journalists who participated in the Irish module.

When asked to place themselves on a scale where 7 is right, 1 is left and 4 is centre, *Irish journalists as a group identified more with the left than with the right.* The Irish,

9 Browne, V. 'The Cardinal: essentially right on the media' in *Sunday Tribune*, 7 June 1992.   10 See Lichter, S.R. & Rothman, S. (1986) *The media elite: America's new power brokers*. Bethesda, MD: Adler and Adler.   11 Kepplinger, H. & Kocher, R. 'Professionalism in the media world.' *European Journal of Communications* 5 (2-3) 1990, 285-312.   12 The study involved the administration of a detailed questionnaire to a national sample of print and broadcast journalists. The questionnaire was originally developed by a team of international scholars led by Tom Patterson of Harvard University and Wolfgang Donsbach of the University of Dresden, as part of a Media and Democracy project conducted in five other countries including Britain, the United States and Germany. An additional module, similar to the one conducted in Ireland, has also been completed in Spain. Issues explored included journalists' rights and responsibilities, their views on freedom of expression and freedom of the press, their attitudes toward the job, and their personal values and political orientations. The target survey population consisted of journalists who are involved in the *daily news process*. In terms of the study a journalist is defined as a person who makes decisions directly affecting daily news content. The category thus includes both reporters and editors. The sole criterion for inclusion is *participation in daily news decisions*. One hundred and nine questionnaires were completed and analyzed using an SPSS package.   13 Patterson, T.E. & Donsbach, W. 'News decisions: journalists as partisan actors'. *Political Communication* (13) 1996 455-68.

TABLE I: THE LEFT–RIGHT POSITIONING (SELF-IDENTIFIED)
OF JOURNALISTS IN SIX COUNTRIES

Italy	Ireland	USA	Germany	Sweden	UK
3.01	3.15	3.32	3.39	3.45	3.46
(1.30)	(1.09)	(1.09)	(1.10)	(1.23)	(1.19)

(Note: figure in brackets denotes standard deviation.)

with a mean score of 3.15, were closest to the Italian journalists (3.01) who were the most liberal group of all those surveyed. British and Swedish journalists with average scores of 3.46 and 3.45, respectively, were the least liberal in orientation. The Irish were also more left leaning that either German (3.39) or U.S. (3.32) journalists. However, the Irish are considerably more moderate than their Italian counterparts. Except in Italy, where 11 per cent of the respondents placed themselves on the far-left position on the 7-point scale, fewer than 5 per cent of the respondents in any country took such a position. Hence, the standard deviation scores are low across all the participant countries on the variable of left / right positioning. Only 3.6 per cent of the Irish journalists placed themselves at the extreme left. Sixty-eight per cent of the Irish sample of daily news producers placed themselves left of centre, and no-one placed themselves on the extreme right. What this suggests is that Irish daily news journalists, across print and broadcast media, are quite moderate in their views tending – like journalists in other countries – to cluster in or around the political centre. This suggests that they are unlikely, even if inclined to adopt an advocacy approach to their journalism, to support extreme positions on either the left or right of the political spectrum.

Media research that has focused on the process of news production within news organizations generally concludes that journalists tend to have a very detached view of their audience. They are most likely to be influenced by their peers within the profession, their close friends, and the institutional culture of which they form part. They are not particularly attuned to the audiences that they serve.[14] Indeed, this 'psychic distance' between journalists and audiences is demonstrated in the significant disjuncture between journalists own self-positioning and where they position their audience in the survey. Journalists in all of the participating countries locate themselves to the left of where they perceive their news audience to be. While on the whole journalists see themselves as slightly left of centre, they locate their audiences as slightly to the right of centre. Interestingly, the difference between journalists' mean position on the 7-point scale and where they positioned their audience was greatest in Ireland where more

14 See, for example, Gans (1980), Tuchman (1978), Epstein (1974), Schlesinger (1978).

than a full point (3.15 and 4.48 respectively) separated the means. The only other country to record such a gap between self-perception and perception of the news organization's audience was the United States (3.32 and 4.47, respectively). The gap between journalists and their news audiences was smallest in Sweden (3.45 and 4.11, respectively) with Italy and Great Britain close behind. In all cases these differences were statistically significant at p<.01. *Irish journalists appear to regard themselves as substantially more liberal than the news audiences that they serve.*

This is born out if we look at the data on party political allegiance. The divergence between journalists and the audiences they serve is most clear-cut when stated political party allegiance is examined. It is particularly instructive to compare this breakdown with data from an *Irish Times*/MRBI opinion poll. The survey of Irish news journalists was carried out between April and September 1997. A general election was held on 7 June 1997. On that morning, the *Irish Times* published a first ever election-day survey that identified (very accurately as it turned out) the first preference positions of the electorate. We can compare data from that public opinion poll with the responses to the question in the study on party preference.

TABLE 2: GENERALLY SPEAKING, WHICH POLITICAL PARTY ARE YOU CLOSER TO?

Party	Frequency	Percentage	*Irish Times-MRBI poll* *Election Day, 7 June 1997*
Fianna Fáil	6	5.6	44
Fine Gael	11	10.3	27
Progressive Democrats	3	2.8	4
Labour Party	37	34.6	11
Green Party	7	6.5	4
No party affiliation	40	37.4	–
Other party	3	2.8	
Missing	2		11
Total	109	100	100

(Note: figures for Democratic Left supporters have been integrated into Labour Party.)

First, it is significant that the largest group – about one third – within the sample of Irish journalists expresses no political affiliation. This clearly demonstrates a strong personal commitment to the idea of impartiality and objectivity that is in keeping with the ethos of professionalism that underlies the modern ideal of journalism. This suggests that a considerable number of journalists across print and broadcast media see no role for themselves as either adversaries of 'the system' or as advocates for particular sectors of the population.

The next largest group (33 per cent) is closest to the Labour Party. Just under 3 per cent were close to the Progressive Democrats and a similar percentage were close to Sinn Féin. Surprisingly, Green Party supporters at 6.3 per cent outnumber supporters of Fianna Fáil – the party receiving just over 5 per cent of support among daily news journalists. Just over 10 per cent of journalists are close to the Fine Gael party. In stark contrast, the June 1997 *Irish Times*-MRBI poll shows 44 per cent electoral support for Fianna Fáil, 27 per cent for Fine Gael, 11 per cent for the Labour Party (inclusive of Democratic Left); 4 per cent for the Progressive Democrats, 4 per cent for the Green Party, and 11 per cent for others. This demonstrates that, in terms of political positioning, there appears to be a gap between the stated political preferences of journalists and those of the audiences they serve. Labour Party supporters are highly over-represented in the media compared to their distribution in the population-at-large. Supporters of the Green Party are also somewhat over-represented. Clearly though, the mainstream parties – and in particular Fianna Fáil – are significantly under-represented in terms of the distribution of their supporters among the national news media. Since the majority of journalists now receive a specialist professional training for the job, and since they generally work for news organizations that have a clearly stated ethos, they are highly constrained in terms of the extent to which they can give voice in their workplace to private political views. Coupled with the fact that about a third of journalists are effectively apolitical, and that most hover around the political centre, we can only conclude that the media in Ireland is largely politically moderate and certainly not given to extreme views. Hence, any rational for censorship based on the unreliability of journalists to deliver the news in a fair and impartial way, seems somewhat misjudged.

REFLEXIVE IRISH AUDIENCES

As we have seen, attempts at censorship are predicated on a view of the audience as infantile, easily manipulated and gullible. Research carried out in Ireland tends to confound these presuppositions. In their 1997 volume, Kelly and O'Connor assembled a rich seam of qualitative research on audiences on the island of Ireland. They demonstrate the manner in which media audiences are subdivided into subcultures based on class, gender and ethnicity. In addition, they point out 'that there is a reflexivity and awareness within these subcultures, especially those less privileged and powerful, that their voices are not frequently heard in the media'.[15]

Watson, for example, demonstrates that a simulated newscast shown to Protestant and Catholics in Northern Ireland elicited a range of different audience

15 Kelly, M. J. & O'Connor, B. (eds) (1997) *Media audiences in Ireland.* Dublin: UCD Press, 12.

responses. In particular, the scheme of interpretation deployed by audience members appeared to mobilise pre-existing belief structures. Furthermore, 'many responses also seemed to be motivated by, and functioned to reaffirm, particular social group interest'.[16] In other words, as audience research elsewhere has demonstrated, ethno-political discourses in which audience members are embedded mediate audiences' responses to television. The 'audience groups through their cultural and social differences were able to generate radically different responses to a single television news programme'.[17] These findings are not particularly surprising given what we have learned from the audience research tradition, particularly over the last twenty or so years. There is a wealth of empirical evidence (that is often overlooked by journalists when they write about media audiences) that demonstrates that people's embeddedness in social networks, access to a range of viewpoints, levels of education, and general civic engagement act as a bulwark against easy manipulation by media messages.

David Miller set out to examine the process by which people come to 'make up their minds' about the conflict in Northern Ireland, by researching audiences in Northern Ireland, Scotland and England between 1988 and 1990. While his research shows that significant numbers of people in Britain believed key elements of the official definition of the conflict in Northern Ireland as a result of media portrayals of that conflict, they did not necessarily come to the same political conclusions as that of the government. British public opinion had been in favour of British withdrawal from Ireland for most of the period between 1972 and 1994. Furthermore, Miller points out that 'political conclusions do not necessarily lead to political action, as can be seen by the lack of support in Britain for organizations openly campaigning for British withdrawal' during that period.[18]

Clearly, how and why the audience responds to particular media messages is shaped at least to some degree, by the social context of reception. The 'dominant ideology' and 'dominant audience' perspectives offer polar opposite interpretations of the relationship between the medium, the message and the audience.[19] No media analyst has yet managed to conclusively endorse either one position or the other. Indeed, the cultural theorist David Morley has argued that 'the history of audience studies during the post-war era can be seen as a series of oscillations between perspectives which have stressed the power of the text or message over the audience and perspectives which have stressed the barriers protecting the audience from the potential effects of the message'.[20]

---

16 Watson, R. 'Northern Ireland audiences and television news' in Kelly, M.J. & O'Connor, B., op. cit., 246–66 at 164.   17 Watson, R. op. cit., 165.   18 Miller, D. 'Dominant ideologies and media power: the case of Northern Ireland' in Kelly, M.J. & O'Connor, B., op. cit., 126–45 at 140.   19 Abercrombie, N. op. cit.   20 Morley, D. (1989) 'Changing paradigms in audience studies' in Seiter, E. et al. (eds) *Remote control: television, audiences and cultural power.* London: Routledge, 16–43 at 16.

To what extend was the audience in the Republic of Ireland politically naive when it came to coverage of 'The Troubles' in Northern Ireland? What did the Irish public think of the provisions of Section 31 when in force, and of how it was applied in practice? To answer these questions I draw on the audience research conducted by Meehan and Horgan at the end of the 1980s when Section 31 was still in force.[21] A sample of 500 randomly selected individuals in the Dublin area responded to a short questionnaire designed to test their awareness of and attitudes towards the Section 31 provision.

Just under two-thirds of those surveyed reported without prompting that they were aware of a law preventing certain groups from being interviewed on RTÉ. Once given a short explanation of Section 31 of the Broadcasting Act, three-quarters of respondents correctly and without prompting identified at least one organization or type of organization as being banned from expressing their views on RTÉ. This shows a relatively high level of political awareness, knowledge and understanding of the issues on the part of the general public.

A majority of respondents – 53 per cent – disapproved of the provision, with opposition concentrated among those under fifty years of age in the lower social class groupings. Despite an overall approval rating of 36 per cent for the Section 31 provision, a large majority of respondents (almost three-quarters) thought that Sinn Féin should be allowed to express its opinion on RTÉ when a news story affected it. An even higher proportion of the respondents (83 per cent) thought that local authority members speaking on local issues and trade union officials speaking on trade union issues who are otherwise subject to Section 31 should be allowed to speak on RTÉ. This clearly shows that the Irish audience as a whole rejects the idea of political censorship, particularly when the censorship provision extends beyond a narrowly defined remit. In other words, the broadcast audience clearly was able to distinguish between political broadcasting that might be used as a platform for promulgating 'extreme' political views, and broadcasting that dealt with non-political issues such as economic welfare, social rights, etc. This was a distinction, which as an institution RTÉ did not make, and which created a 'chilling effect' on coverage of any issue that had the remotest connection to a proscribed organization. Just under 80 per cent of respondents said they wanted to be explicitly informed by RTÉ when Section 31 had affected the making of a programme. Overall, the findings of the Meehan and Horgan study point to an audience that is engaged by political subject matter, that understands the contentious issue of censorship, and that is capable of providing nuanced and reflective responses. Hence, the survey tends to support

21 Meehan, N. & Horgan, J. (1989) *Survey on attitudes of the Dublin population to Section 31 of the Broadcasting Act.* Dublin: National Institute for Higher Education.

the dominant audience view that a critical reading of messages emanating from the mass media is possible.

Audience research has served to muddy rather than clarify the debate in relation to media effects. This makes it very difficult to pronounce on the characteristics as such of the mass audience. In reality, people tend to bring their own pre-existing opinions, beliefs and prejudices with them when they come to watch television or listen to the radio. Depending on the content of the media (whether it is news or entertainment, whether it is about issues of immediate or remote concern) and the context of reception (the level and intensity of the audience's attention, the level of personal interest, knowledge and motivation) our pre-existing beliefs may be reinforced or challenged. What is important to remember is that the audience is not an undifferentiated and homogenous mass that will always react in a uniform and predictable way.

And yet, the way in which audiences have been constructed by legislators in Ireland, historically and to the present day, has stubbornly clung to the idea of the national audience as easily manipulated and susceptible to undesirable influences emanating from the media. But to subscribe to an easily influenced audience one must concomitantly subscribe to a notion of an all-powerful media. As James Hawthorne has pointed out: 'The power of the media resides in the widespread belief that it is all powerful and in our fear of its ability to persuade and to undermine the public's capacity to think for itself.'[22] Forms of information control, however innocuous and necessary they may appear, always have the effect of infantilising the audience. The message they send out is that we are not capable of making up our minds for ourselves. In other words, 'the belief in information freedom is based on the maturity of those who enjoy it; limitations betray a belief that people are not capable of judging between right or wrong, and that broadcasters are similarly deficient or given to propaganda'.[23]

CONCLUSION

The conceptualization and implementation of Section 31 was predicated on a particular set of assumptions: that censorship is sometimes necessary to protect the body politic, that journalists must therefore be restrained in carrying out their work, and that what the audience don't know won't hurt them. Here I have argued that these premises are questionable if not downright false. While Irish journalists in the main hold liberal views, they are positioned only slightly to the left of centre. Journalists strongly subscribe to the notion of impartiality and consider

22 Dr James Hawthorne, former controller of the BBC in Northern Ireland (quoted in the *Irish Times*, 3 August 1992).
23 *Irish Times* editorial, 'A blunt instrument', 11 June 1991.

themselves as professionals in their work. Irish audiences appear to have been well informed and discerning on the issue of Section 31 and its remit.

But what is it that governments that engage in censorship are trying to protect? And how viable is the project of censorship in a world where time and space differences are being obliterated by the sheer flow of information through multiple media platforms? The notions of 'a national audience' and 'a body politic' are increasingly questionable in a media-saturated world. According to Stevenson, a number of key features shape the contemporary relationship between the public and the mass media.[24] Firstly, for most of us most of the time we engage with the media in privatised contexts where we are rendered largely passive. The media's capacity to make us aware of common concerns (for example, the global news reach of the story of the September 11th attacks on the Twin Towers in New York City) is mitigated to some degree by the comparative isolation in which we make our interpretations. There are fewer and fewer opportunities or avenues through which people may pursue a collective response to either the terrorist attacks or to the US retaliation – we feel pretty powerless – and maybe even fearful – a lot of the time. Furthermore, greater fragmentation of the media audience means that rather than constituting a national audience of citizens we are increasingly composed of targeted audience segments, served up to advertisers and programme sponsors. The idea of a national audience being preserved from the views of proscribed political parties seems somewhat archaic from the perspective of 2004, when more and more people live in multi-channel, multi-platform land. As Stevenson asserts, the very fragmentation of the national audience makes it more difficult for governments and information managers to control and censor debate: 'The rapid expansion of new media made available by technological change will mean that our public culture will become increasingly based on individual choice in ways that are poorly appreciated by the mass culture thesis.'[25]

Secondly, the rapid development of media technologies has increased the volume of information available. But more information does not necessarily mean a more informed citizenry. Indeed, Peillon has described how the use of public opinion polls and mass surveys by the political class (and increasingly by media professionals) enables them 'to remain within the confines of a predictable public opinion in order to find its political action validated, justified'.[26] In other words, the audience can become 'the news' through extensive use of opinion polls, exit polls, straw polls, email and so on. The delivery of information is now almost simultaneous and a wealth of new interactive mechanisms is available to news producers and their audiences through the internet. Indeed, the internet helps to

24 Stevenson, N. (1999) *The transformation of the media: globalisation, morality and ethics.* London: Longman.   25 Stevenson, op. cit.   26 Peillon, M. 'Information overload' in Peillon, M. & Slater, E. (eds) (2000) *Memories of the present.* Dublin: Institute of Public Administration, 165–83 at 181.

blur the distinction between producer and consumer since it facilitates two-way interactions. If one cannot source a story through the mainstream media, it is always possible to source it through the multiple outlets providing a range of alternative perspectives on the internet. However, there is also the problem of information overload. How many of us have felt increasingly desensitised to the stories emanating from Iraq as we struggle to digest the information avalanche?

Right across Europe we have witnessed the erosion of the commitment to public service broadcasting, as the commercial imperative comes to dominate. And if there is no longer a place for public service broadcasting, is there a place for the public sphere? Even in countries like Britain, where public service broadcasting has historically been strong, it has been subjected to a bruising. The Hutton Inquiry in Britain may turn out to mark a watershed in terms of the relationship between government and public service broadcasting. The BBC, an institution trusted and respected all over the world, found itself in the dock while a government that led Britain to war on the basis of what turned out to be false information, was exonerated. Accusations of a 'whitewash' quickly circulated in the media, as pundits grappled with the idea that the messenger rather than the message had been well and truly shot. What all the commentators agree on, however, is the fact that the audience is as ever astute and discerning. 'YouGov' polls conducted for the *Daily Telegraph* in the aftermath of Hutton showed that 56 per cent of respondents agreed that the Hutton Report was a whitewash and less than a third trusted Ministers to tell the truth.[27] In other words, Mr Blair may have found favour with Lord Hutton and won the battle with the BBC, but he has not won over public opinion. The audience may yet bite back.

27 Ranwnsley, A. 'A messy draw' in *Observer*, 1 February 2004.

10 / Culture, democracy and public service broadcasting

MICHAEL D. HIGGINS

The times through which we are now living are for many people who gave, and give, their energies to the public world, times of considerable pessimism. It is as if what is happening constitutes an imperceptible drift away from policy, from ideas, from philosophies. It is a condition that writers such as Charles Taylor, describe as a drift to *unfreedom*.[1] I believe the manner in which we are uncritically accepting unaccountable markets as a substitute for accountable public policy represents one of the most serious aspects of this drift away from democracy. Indeed, I believe we are now living through the early stages of a deep enslavement. It is a historical moment of the greatest importance – our retreat from the public world, our substitution of existence as consumers for an active life as citizens, our definition of our world as a world of private consumption, our surrender on terms we neither understand nor have negotiated, to the market.

THE RETREAT FROM THE PUBLIC WORLD

The loss of the public world is being experienced through the subjugation of the cultural space to a set of economic policies derived historically from a very narrow ideological furrow – the adherents of Van Hayek and the New Right. It is a time of the greatest pessimism for even such distinguished historians of, and contributors to, public service broadcasting, as Michael Tracey whose seminal work *The Decline and Fall of Public Service Broadcasting* charts the story of broadcasting right up to its present time of crisis.[2] Broadcasting now stands to be judged as a production space for commodified entertainment products rather than that public space where citizens listened and viewed to be informed, educated, or entertained.

We spend a great deal of our conscious life watching and listening to what is broadcast. The late and great Raymond Williams gave as the title to his last paper 'Be The Arrow Not The Target'. When I as Minister for Arts, Culture and the Gaeltacht with responsibility for broadcasting in the mid-1990s was publishing a Green Paper on the future of broadcasting in Ireland, I had this title in mind when

1 Taylor, C. (1991) *The ethics of authenticity*. Cambridge, Mass.: Harvard University Press.   2 Tracey, M. (1998) *The decline and fall of public service broadcasting*. Oxford: Oxford University Press.

I called the Green Paper *Broadcasting in the Future Tense: Active or Passive?* From when I read his work for the first time in the late 1950s or early 1960s I was moved by Raymond Williams' commitment to public education and to the role of the media in the deepening, widening, and enriching of the life of the public. That public world in which there was a connection between philosophy and politics, between ethics and economics, between culture and public service broadcasting is under severe threat. Everywhere we look, that public world with its tradition of public space and service is slipping away. The losers will not only be broadcasters and their audiences but the wider fabric of the society, across a long spectrum of time, which may not be able to recover the values it is now near unconsciously losing. In the course of his discussion on the BBC, Michael Tracey makes reference to the key principles of public service broadcasting, which are worth reproducing here: universality of availability; universality of appeal; provision for minorities, especially those disadvantaged by physical or social circumstance; service the public' sphere – the nation speaking to itself; commitment to the education of the public distance from all vested interests; structured so as to encourage competition in good programming rather than competition for numbers; and the rules of broadcasting should *liberate rather than restrict* the programme-maker.[3] It is easy to see how such principles fit within a model of active participatory and democratic citizenship. It is equally clear that they do not constitute an agenda that would be accepted readily by those who are providing produce for the commercial audiovisual market at the present time. Nor are they always readily acceptable to national governments that may, under certain circumstances, seek to shape the content of public service broadcasting in particular ways, as several of the contributions in this book demonstrate.

THE COMMERCIAL IMPERATIVE

The issue of the licence fee as a source of funding was closely linked to the notion of community and what citizens held in common. It was not merely symbolic, although it might have been on the public service channels that one expected coverage of the great events and personages of one's time. There was a sense in which the licence fee funded the public service broadcasting system, a system that contributed to cohesion, integration and a sense of identity. Ireland has had both the challenge and the benefit of being a next-door neighbour to the BBC. Indeed there are times when one can detect the ghost of Lord Reith in some of the statements of those given charge of Irish broadcasting. In more recent times I recall the Chairman of RTÉ of the day describing RTÉ to me as a business with so many thou-

3 Broadcasting Research Unit principles of public service broadcasting quoted in ibid.

sand employees. I always refer to it as the national broadcaster. However, this precise shift from national broadcaster to large commercial unit with thousands of employees mirrored what had happened in Britain since the deregulation of the 1980s, a policy shift that totally changed the character of British broadcasting. The ethos forced on public service broadcasting in Britain was itself born in an anti-state enterprise environment pioneered by Margaret Thatcher. Reflecting on these changes and the current media environment, I have come to the conclusion that the only sure rock upon which the future of public service broadcasting might be built is one that puts the programme makers at the centre of things, that is suspicious of alleged technical managerial expertise, and that pursues the truth, *without internal or external constraint.* If the absence of public understanding is losing some support for public service broadcasting, I also have the feeling that the subjugation of broadcasting values to organisational ones is part of a more generalized loss of confidence that is now so blatantly clear in society.

In recent years of course, there has been a fundamental and rapid change in technology. This has represented a particular kind of seduction. Many politicians seem lost in awe or their eyes glaze over at the mention of the digital super highway. It is as if it all were too exciting, too promising as a competitive tool in the market to be made amenable to regulation. If the technology has arrived with rapidity the issue as to how it should be applied, has, however, generated a deadly silence. Yet how this matter is handled will decide whether we deepen and widen communications or whether we open up a new fissure in society between the information rich and the information poor. The European Union is a good example of how those anxious to make profit from 'new services' have, with the assistance of the Commission, steam rolled over those interested in securing the future of public service broadcasting and an accountability to the public from those who have constructed new monopolies. Put bluntly, the Commission has worked very hard at deregulating public service broadcasting, but despite pressure from the European Parliament again and again, it has refused to bring in a Directive on concentration of ownership, something that is increasing every day. Those who support public service broadcasting are sometimes pilloried as backward traditionalists, old regulationists, standing in the way of the shining future with new services. In Europe today nearly every country – including the accession countries – is preparing or drafting broadcasting legislation that will attempt to strike a balance with the market place. In nearly every country the hard technology of communications is seeking to establish a hegemony over what is perceived to be the softer cultural target of broadcasting within culture. This issue arises regularly over such issues as whether there should be a different regulator for content and mode of delivery. These are not just issues as to political turf. Behind them there is a huge body of investment whose short-term profit may require the public interest to be forgotten.

The main tendencies in communications at the present time include convergence of technology, concentration of ownership in a number of international conglomerates and fragmentation of audiences. These tendencies occur at a time when the prevailing ideology guiding economic policy decisions is one that places an emphasis on unrestricted market adjustments. The circumstances of these transitions are different from other historical shifts of the industrial era. It is very difficult to question, indeed identify, the assumptions, upon which they are based. We are drifting into, rather than choosing, this new condition of our unfreedom — *our existence as consumers rather than citizens.* Citizenship, the public space, the shared moment, the common history, the shared community of the imagination are all perceived as tired old phrases. Interests are what have to be addressed. A private world of consumer choice and its advertisements have replaced an older but still necessary debate about adequate provision in the public space. With these shifts in private consumption it is arguable if there is any real meaning to our use of the word culture at all. When a lifestyle is that to which we aspire, cultural product has a meaning quite different, a mode of production quite different, from any previous concept of shared meaning. It is when we are alone, consuming privately, consumed in our consumption, we experience a peculiarly new form of alienation and loneliness. We seek relief from the television. We are open to be entertained. We are willing to subscribe to be entertained. Indeed the smart box on the television may take the thinking out of it for us altogether. There are rare exceptions to this — moments when the public world is rediscovered. I was moved by the account given by Michael Tracey of the forty-eight hours around the death of President John F. Kennedy when advertisements disappeared and a vast diverse community shared a moment of grief.[4] It was a public moment to which immense personal emotion was brought by so many — becoming part of the collative memory.

VALUING THE PUBLIC SPHERE

At the bases of the choices we will make in the next few years are some fundamental value choices involving such questions as — What value do we put on the public world? — What value do we put on issues beyond the immediate, beyond a single life span? — How do we wish to remember and be remembered? — What do we wish to be free to imagine? Such value choices raise questions about the cultural space, its relationship to the economic space, how it is to be defined, is it to be open or closed, democratic or autocratic, fixed by tradition or flexible to the contemporary and the as yet unremembered. In a curious way there has always been public support for a definition of culture that would have critical capacity

4 Tracey, M., op. cit.

at its centre. Those who made programmes knew that sometimes their work would strike a strange resonance with the past, sometimes it would be anticipatory in its innovation. Nothing was really predictable but the standard had to have, as its basic, *respect for freedom and creativity*. This has been brought into sharp relief for me in my role as a public representative. I had debated the advisability of introducing the Section 31 order in the Oireachtas in 1975. By a strange coincidence, almost twenty years later, I found myself in a position as Minister for Arts, Culture and the Gaeltacht with responsibility for broadcasting, to rescind that order. I would like to take this opportunity to share with you my sense of the issues – dealt with at length in this book – from a politician's perspective.

The debate on broadcasting that took place in Seanad Éireann in 1975, in which Dr Conor Cruise O'Brien introduced some fundamental changes in broadcasting in Ireland, was one of the most thorough examinations of broadcasting, in my time in the Oireachtas. It was informed and elegant. It is also clear from the report of that debate that while Dr O'Brien and I agreed on many things we differed in relation to the freedom that should be accorded to the broadcaster. Dr O'Brien stressed the importance of public order. I, admitting to be attracted to 'philosophical anarchy', asked him to look again at the Section which introduced restrictions, as I saw it, that could be tantamount to censorship. Much of Dr O'Brien's presentation in what was a brilliant speech concentrated on what he felt to be the limits of liberalism:

> Unfortunately, the wish to be liberal, or to demand liberalism from others, is often accompanied by only the vaguest notions of what liberalism is, as the slogans about repressive legislation show. The debate now opening would be particularly useful if it helped clarify ideas in that regard. The simple principle which came to be at the heart of the liberal democratic state was laid down for Athens more than 2,000 years ago: 'neither excessive rule nor anarchy that is the mean my townsmen shall observe'.[5]

Here, Dr O'Brien was quoting from the *Oresteia* of Aeschylus in support of his argument for limitations on freedom of expression. Almost twenty years later, the debate was still going strong. In the interim, before I decided to end the order that forbade interviews with such people as members of Sinn Féin, it was clear to me that the argument had not fundamentally changed. The kernel of the issue was as to whether protection of the public required a restriction of broadcasting, or whether such a proscription constituted censorship. I held the latter view. I saw it as indicating a lack of trust in the broadcaster, in those who had the editorial control, and above all, of the public's capacity to discriminate.

5 See the chapter by Conor Cruise O'Brien, above.

When I became Minister for Arts, Culture and the Gaeltacht with responsibility for broadcasting I saw this issue as one of censorship. My thinking on it, while taking account of the conflict in Northern Ireland, was not governed by such a consideration. I was appointed Minister with responsibility for Broadcasting in January 1993. My predecessor Máire Geoghegan Quinn had refused to meet the NUJ and renewed the order as one of her last acts, prior to handing over to me.[6] During the year that followed I consulted with many groups but by now was dealing with the impatience of some of those who shared my views as to the abolition of the order. Appearing on *Questions and Answers* within a couple of weeks of my appointment, my reply to the extent that I was consulting with individuals and groups drew the response from Nell McCafferty – 'What has happened my beautiful Michael D?' Later, on my attendance at a poetry reading in Cork, after the launch of my volume *Season of Fire*, I saw the Special Branch standing in front of Sinn Féin protestors as I went in to read. In Galway my publisher headed a little protest before he accompanied me to my reading – a fact that dominated one of the reviews of my collection of poems. It was not an easy time. I could have gone to government with a paper proposing a government decision – seeking to revoke the Section 31 order – satisfied my new critics, and lost. Nevertheless, I do understand the latter's position. At cabinet and senior level in the Labour Party there was no great anxiety to introduce this topic – proposing that Section 31 not be renewed was described to me by a senior person as akin to 'bungee-jumping'.

On 15 December 1993 at Question Time in the Dáil I was questioned by Frances Fitzgerald of Fine Gael and Pat Rabbitte of Democratic Left as to my intentions. I replied that there would be no automatic renewal of the order and stated that I had 'asked the RTÉ authority to have the guidelines ready which they would propose to issue to staff in the event that the order under Section 31 was not renewed'. By now I had circulated a Paper proposing a government decision on the issue of non-renewal of the order to my colleagues in government and, while I am precluded from giving details, I should say that the Department of Justice was the Department from which I expected opposition. In the event, the Minister for Justice, my predecessor in Broadcasting, was in Canada when the decision not to renew the order was taken, in January 1994. I recall the events that followed very clearly. As so many requests had been received for interview I decided to give all the interviews from my office in the Department at Mespil Road. Very early on, word came that the British Ambassador was downstairs seeking a copy of the Broadcasting Act that contained the provisions for the Section 31 order. A senior official told me that I was under no obligation to accede to his

6 See the chapter by Alex White above for details of the legal basis and workings of Section 31.

rather abrupt demands. Nevertheless, I gave instructions for a copy of the Act to be made for Mr Blatherwick. I recall him popping his head around the door and his suggesting that he was getting the next plane to London. I wished him God speed. The following Wednesday I met my opposite number, the British Minister of State, who told me he had been instructed to remonstrate with me for the absence of prior consultation, but who, over coffee, confirmed that he would be doing the same thing that I had in relation to the British broadcasting ban.

At this stage I should say that while it was clear to me that Bob Collins[7] and other senior people at RTÉ, including Joe Barry,[8] were in favour of ending the order, there were significant others who were in favour of keeping it and others again who had adjusted themselves to living within it, for whom it made life easy. So while the majority appeared to hold an anti-censorship view I was in no doubt of the existence of a group that was happy to live with the organizational neatness of a prohibition. Not having to exercise discretion always helps the dedicated organizational person.

In the Dáil debate that followed, Michael McDowell moved a motion on 1 February 1994, criticising my decision not to renew the order.[9] In the course of his speech he stated:

> The Progressive Democrats do not believe that Section 31 is, as the Minister seems to have believed for many years past, an issue of political censorship or an issue in which freedom of speech arises.

Robert Molloy was even more direct:

> The Minister in his contribution yesterday chose to deal with Section 31 as though it were an issue in which the rights of people to information and the rights of people to speak were in some sense at odds with the security interests of the state. This Minister, posing as a liberal, has asked this house to welcome to the airwaves members of a subversive revolutionary movement who, day in day out, use murder as part of its stock in trade.

This assertion was of course outrageous, harking back to Conor Cruise O'Brien's argument almost twenty years earlier that 'excessive' liberalism could not go unchecked in a modern democratic state. Jim O'Keeffe of Fine Gael also disagreed with me:

> The Minister, Deputy Higgins, talks about it being a question of the basic issue of freedom of information and expression versus censorship. That is

7 Then Deputy Director General of RTÉ.   8 Then Director General of RTÉ.   9 *Dáil Éireann Debates* 438 (1994) cols. 209–45 & 538–76.

where we part company. I do not see that as the issue. The issue, as far as I am concerned, is whether Sinn Féin, the IRA, or the groups covered by the order, were to be allowed access to the airwaves to spread their message of violence and to be given an opportunity to dispense propaganda. The maturity of the people is not an issue, nor is the professionalism of the broadcasting media and journalists. Propaganda is very subtle. If these people come on the airwaves openly advocating violence they will be stopped but that is not how propaganda operates. It is an art which is central to the whole process as far as Sinn Féin and the IRA are concerned.

The amendment moved in my name on behalf of the government rejected Deputy McDowell's criticism of me for not renewing the order.[10] Thus, my decision was affirmed by 79 votes to 43. A number of years later, I would return to the theme in preparing legislation on broadcasting. By March 1997, I was in the final stages of a Broadcasting Bill – a Green Paper *Broadcasting in the Future Tense* and Heads of Legislation *Clear Focus* having been published previously. I remained of the opinion that Section 31 was unnecessary and planned to abolish Section 31 completely in the proposed Broadcasting Act. All the old opponents remained and indeed, I recall the terms of compromises being discussed with such as the Department of Justice. Making the renewal of the order not automatic as it was, but requiring the assent of the Oireachtas and explanation of the reasons why it should be invoked, removed what the Department of Justice felt was their flexibility and their ability to act quickly in a crisis situation. Officials felt not only Section 31's necessity but were also reluctant to accept the discipline of a prior Dáil debate, approval and later evaluation.

By now I was leaving government. Certainly the removal of the order had an effect on the Northern Ireland talks. Much more importantly, the people's right to exercise their own discretion and judgment had been partially vindicated. The removal of self-censorship would be a longer journey. For me, the removal of the order and the establishment of Teilifís na Gaeilge are probably the two issues that constituted what one might call bottom lines. Both issues pertained to the notion of the public sphere and a civic culture in which all shades of opinion – representing dominant groups and minority groups as well as official, alternative and oppositional voices – might be represented.

---

10 The amendment stated: That Dáil Éireann, recognising the maturity of the Irish people, welcomes the Government decision not to renew the Order under Section 31 (1) of the Broadcasting Authority (Amendment) Acts 1960 to 1993 and expresses confidence in the professionalism of Irish broadcast media journalists in carrying out their responsibilities in compliance with the terms of Article 40 of the Constitution, the Prohibition of Incitement to Hatred Act 1989 and current broadcasting legislation.

THE FUTURE OF BROADCASTING

Professor Farrel Corcoran has written of the voyeuristic culture than can be exploited as a substitute for news or current affairs, and the paucity of party political debate:

> Television schedules flirt with soft porn, celebrate gross consumption, glorify guns and demonise all the wretched of the earth. The relentless earnings pressure of commercial broadcasting makes programming just another corporate operation, driven by the same demands of the financial market as steel making, banking or fast food merchandising.[11]

Professor Corcoran saw as the source of the reduction of the standard among other things the fact that 'too few people make decisions about what the population needs to know, resulting in a one dimensional smooth edged cultural flow that colonizes the national symbolic environment'.[12]

If the public space, and public service broadcasting is part of it, is lessened, there will be an immense social loss at the level of integration, cohesion, and sense of community. If there is a loss of discourse through public service broadcasting; if it is accompanied by low turn-out in elections, low political participation, the emergence of, as it were, an etiquette of being apolitical, then the confrontation between the beneficiaries and the losers of the market will, in the decades to come be unmeditated by institutions such as trade unions and political parties. Such confrontations, without a mediating discourse, will carry a far greater risk of violence. Public service broadcasting is important then. It is important that it continue to enjoy widespread public support. Indeed, many of those who are opposed to the concept of the public service broadcaster are willing to retain the concept of public service broadcasting itself.

The definition of public service broadcasting and of the public service broadcaster is a matter of some importance. To me, the structure of the public space across the programming schedules is what is important. The broadcaster has to be assessed by the totality and the philosophy of content. The issue is not one of having a sprinkling of one of the eight values we mentioned at the outset. It is how all of these are achieved continuously for a significant proportion of the public in a universal way. One of the important benefits of having a vibrant public service broadcasting arrangement is that in addition to inviting citizens to experience the timeless, the universal, the unimagined, it is also a rich source of

---

11 Corcoran, F. 'The future of public service broadcasting in the single audio visual market'. Paper presented to an informal meeting of the Ministers of the European Union with responsibility for culture and audio-visual matters, September 1996.   12 Ibid.

creativity — a creativity that is not confined to the broadcasting station or to one activity. We have arrived at a situation in which it is perfectly clear that public service broadcasting will exist in future in a mixed model of broadcasting. If it is the strong partner in such a mixed model, if it itself values creativity and programme making as its principal definition of itself, it will have a positive effect as to standards on its partners within the mixed model. If it is the weaker partner it will seek to compete with what surrounds it and will embark, perhaps even imperceptibly, on a process of self-commercialisation with the downgrading of programme making and an obsessive, market-led, concentration on programme acquisition and provision.

Public service broadcasting is often viewed as an anachronism in today's media landscape. I believe, that public service broadcasting, unambiguously funded by the licence fee — an important practical and emblematic bond with the citizen — can be a powerful space of creativity. The importance of creativity is enhanced rather than lessened in a model of mixed production. There is an interaction of standards that is most important for the overall quality of the broadcasting that emerges. It is from an atmosphere like this that many learn what they will later use for a source of innovation in the cultural industries. In this space it becomes clear that, rather than it being the case that we must wait for the surpluses of the economic space to allow cultural events to happen, and cultural products to emerge, it is the case that economics can be made human again by being made creative. I am convinced that we need regulation in the digital age if there is to be the diversity that the technology promises — the twin tendencies of unregulated concentration of ownership and fragmentation of audiences promise disaster. There will be of course, always, a need for broadcasting, while being provided for from the licence fee, for example, to have its freedom respected if it is to achieve its critical role in society. The state's role is neither neutral nor residual, but if it is to be interventionist that intervention should be in a manner than confers *freedom with responsibility*.

In conclusion then, there is a new communications order on our planet, but one that works in a very uneven and unfair fashion. The great majority of the world's citizens are reduced by it to the condition of consumers — and what they mainly consume are visual images, sometimes woeful misrepresentations of themselves, coming from one particular part of the planet, the United States, and indeed from just one subsection of that mighty country. The choice is as to whether we become the consumers of images in a passive culture or the makers of images in an active culture in a democratic society. It will ultimately prove futile to seek to create boundaries, barriers and checkpoints in an age of transnational electronic media. The more unified and homogenous our political structures become, the more will people turn to indigenous cultures for an expression of themselves. Now more than ever, we need to cleave to the principles underlying public broadcasting and the public sphere. Benjamin Barber warns of a world dominated by two ideologies, Jihad and McWorld, which are united in their indifference to civil liberties:

> Jihad forges communities of blood rooted in exclusion and hatred, communities that slight democracy in favour of tyrannical paternalism or consensual tribalism. McWorld forges global markets rooted in consumption and profit, leaving to an untrustworthy, if not altogether fictitious, invisible hand issues of public interest and common goods that once might have been nurtured by democratic citizenries and their watchful governments. [...] Today ... we seem intent on recreating a world in which our only choices are the secular universalism of the cosmopolitan market and the everyday particularism of the fractious tribe.[13]

Professor Barber's analysis may be somewhat apocalyptic but it does stress the important issues of identity and diversity. With digitalization comes an entirely new set of policy decisions that policy makers cannot avoid. For example, there will be competition between political providers as to mode of delivery. It will be important to insist that content is even more important than capacity. The debate cannot afford to be exclusively technical except at a huge democratic cost. Blurring the values content of the new revolution suits the conglomerates that benefit from a concentration of ownership as much as it weakens citizenship. The shared space will come under threat and we should remember the injunction that we should humanize goings-on in the world and within ourselves by speaking of it, and in the course of speaking about it, learn to be fully human. We live by stories, and the principles by which stories are selected, the skill with which they are told and their resonance or otherwise in our own culture is a fundamental democratic concern.

13 Barber, B. (1996) *Jihad vs. McWorld.* New York: Ballantine Books.

Bibliography

Abercrombie, N. (1996) *Television and society*. Cambridge: Polity Press.

Adams, M. (1968) *Censorship: the Irish experience*. University, Alabama: University of Alabama Press.

Allen, G. (1999) *The Garda Síochána: policing independent Ireland, 1922–82*. Dublin: Gill and Macmillan.

Andrews, C.S. (1982) *Man of no property*. Dublin: Mercier Press.

Barber, B. (1996) *Jihad vs. McWorld*. New York: Ballantine Books.

Chubb, B. (1974) *The government and politics of Ireland*. Oxford: Oxford University Press.

Corcoran, F. (2004) *RTÉ and the globalisation of Irish television*. Bristol: Intellect.

Curtis, L. (1984) *Ireland: The propaganda war*. London: Pluto Press.

Davis, E. & Sinnott, R. (1979) *Attitudes in the Republic of Ireland relevant to the Northern Ireland problem: Volume 1: Descriptive analysis and some comparisons with attitudes in Northern Ireland and Great Britain*. Dublin: Economic and Social Research Institute.

Doolan, L., Dowling, J. and Quinn, B. (1969) *Sit down and be counted: the cultural evolution of a television station*. Dublin: Wellington Publishers.

Doornaert, M. & Larsen, H. (1987) *Censoring the 'Troubles': an Irish solution to an Irish problem? Report of an IFJ fact-finding mission to Ireland, January 1987*. Brussels: International Federation of Journalists.

Dunne, D. & Kerrigan, G. (1984) *Round up the usual suspects*. Dublin: Magill.

Epstein, E. (1974) *News from nowhere: television and the news*. Chicago: Ivan. R. Dee.

Feeney, P. (1984) 'Censorship and RTÉ'. *The Crane Bag*, 8 (2).

Fennell, D. (1993) *Heresy: the battle of ideas in modern Ireland*. Belfast: Blackstaff Press.

Fisher, D. (1978) *Broadcasting in Ireland*. London: Routledge.

FitzGerald, G. (1991) *All in a life: an autobiography*. Dublin: Gill and Macmillan.

Gans, H. (1980) *Deciding what's news*. London: Constable.

Hall, W. (1993) *The electronic age*. Dublin: Oak Tree Press.

Horgan, J. (1997) *Sean Lemass: the pragmatic patriot*. Dublin: Gill and Macmillan.

Horgan, J. (2001) *Irish media: a critical history since 1922*. London: Routledge.

Horgan, J. (2002) 'Journalists and censorship: a case history of the NUJ in Ireland and the broadcasting ban, 1971–1994'. *Journalism Studies*, 3 (3) Routledge.

Horgan, J. (2004) *Broadcasting and public life: RTÉ news and current affairs*. Dublin: Four Courts Press.

Kelly, M.J. & O'Connor, B. (eds) (1997) *Media audiences in Ireland*. Dublin: UCD Press.

Kenny, C. (1994) 'Section 31 and the censorship of programmes'. *Irish Law Times and Solicitors' Journal*, (n.s) 12 (3).

Kepplinger, H. & Kocher, R. (1990) 'Professionalism in the media world?' *European Journal of Communications*, 5 (2–3).

Lazarsfeld, P. et al. (1948) *The people's choice: how the voter makes up his mind in a presidential campaign*. Columbia: Columbia University Press.

Lippman, W. (1922) *Public opinion*. New York: Macmillan.

Mac Manais, R. (2003) *Maire Mac Giolla Iosa: Breathaisneis*. Galway: Cló Ian-Chonnachta.

McDermott, L. (1996) 'The political censorship of the Irish broadcast media, 1960–1994'. MA thesis, Department of Communications and Theater, Notre Dame University, Indiana.

McGonagle, M. (2002) *Media law*. Dublin: Thompson Round Hall.

Meehan, N. & Horgan, J. (1987) *Survey on attitudes of Dublin population to Section 31 of the Broadcasting Act*. Dublin: National Institute of Higher Education.

Miller, D. (1994) *Don't mention the war: Northern Ireland, propaganda and the media*. London: Pluto Press.

Miller, D. (1994) *Rethinking Northern Ireland: culture, ideology and colonialism*. London: Longman.

Miller, D. (1997) 'Dominant ideologies and media power: the case of Northern Ireland' in Kelly, M.J. & O'Connor, B., op. cit.

Moloney, E. (2002) *A secret history of the IRA*. London: Allen Lane.

Ni Dhonnchadha, M. & Dorgan, T. (eds) (1991) *Revising the Rising*. Derry: Field Air.

'No comment: censorship, secrecy and the Irish Troubles' (1989) *Article 19*, London: International Centre on Censorship.

Noelle-Neumann, E. (1993) *The spiral of silence: public opinion - our social skin*. Chicago: University of Chicago Press.

O'Briain Report (1978) *Report of the Committee to Recommend Certain Safeguards for Persons in Custody and for Members of An Garda Síochána*. Dublin: Stationary Office.

O'Brien, C.C. (1972) *States of Ireland*. London: Hutchinson.

O'Brien, C.C. (1978) *Herod: reflections on political violence*. London: Hutchinson.

O'Brien, C.C. (1998) *Memoir: my life and themes*. Dublin: Poolbeg Press.

O'Brien, J. (2000) *The Arms Trial*. Dublin: Gill and Macmillan.

O'Brien, M. (2001) *De Valera, Fianna Fáil and the* Irish Press*: the truth in the news?* Dublin: Irish Academic Press.

O'Drisceoil, D. (1996) *Censorship in Ireland 1939–1945: neutrality, politics and society*. Cork: Cork University Press.

O'Higgins, P. (1973) 'The Irish TV sackings'. *Index on Censorship*, 2 (1).

Patterson, T.E. & Donsbach, W. (1996) 'News decisions: journalists as partisan actors'. *Political Communication*, 13.

Peillon, M. (2000) 'Information overload' in Peillon, M. & Slater, E. (eds) *Memories of the present*. Dublin: Institute of Public Administration.

Rolston, B. (1991) *The media and Northern Ireland: covering the Troubles*. London: Macmillan.

Rolston, B. & Miller, D. (eds) (1996) *War and words: the Northern Ireland media reader*. Belfast: Beyond the Pale Publications.

Schlesinger, P. (1978) *Putting reality together*: BBC news. London: Constable.

Smyth, P. & Hazelkorn, E. (eds) (1993) *Let in the light: censorship, secrecy and democracy*. Dingle: Brandon.

Stevenson, N. (1999) *The transformation of the media: globalisation, morality and ethics*. London: Longman.

Taylor, C. (1991) *The ethics of authenticity*. Cambridge, Mass.: Harvard University Press.

Tracey, M. (1998) *The decline and fall of public service broadcasting*. Oxford: Oxford University Press.

Tuchman, G. (1978) *Making news: a study in the construction of reality*. New York: Free Press.

Watson, R. (1997) 'Northern Ireland audiences and television news' in Kelly, M.J. & O'Connor, B., op. cit.

Woodman, K. (1985) *Media control in Ireland, 1923–1983*. Carbondale: Southern Illinois University Press.

Index